KT-224-227

# CONTENTS

## Part Three – Meditation in Daily Life

102 045 481 4

T

Sheffield Hallam University
Learning and Information Services
Withdrawn From Stock

# TEACH YOURSELF TO
# Meditate

*Over 20 Simple Exercises for Peace,*
*Health and Clarity of Mind*

# ERIC HARRISON

piatkus

PIATKUS

First published in Australasia in 1993 by Simon & Schuster Australia
First published in Great Britain in 1994 by Piatkus
Reprinted 1994 (twice), 1995, 1996 (three times), 1997 (twice),
1998, 1999 (twice), 2000 (twice), 2001 (three times), 2002, 2005,
2006, 2007, 2009, 2010 (twice), 2011 (twice), 2012 (twice), 2013,
2014 (twice)

Copyright © 1993 by Eric Harrison

The moral right of the author has been asserted.

All rights reserved.
No part of this publication may be reproduced, stored in a
retrieval system, or transmitted, in any form or by any means, without
the prior permission in writing of the publisher, nor be otherwise circulated
in any form of binding or cover other than that in which it is published
and without a similar condition including this condition being
imposed on the subsequent purchaser.

A CIP catalogue record for this book
is available from the British Library.

ISBN 978-0-7499-1328-1

Printed and bound by CPI Group (UK) Ltd, Croydon, CR0 4YY

Papers used by Piatkus are from well-managed forests
and other responsible sources.

MIX
Paper from
responsible sources
FSC
www.fsc.org    FSC® C104740

Piatkus
An imprint of
Little, Brown Book Group
100 Victoria Embankment
London EC4Y 0DY

An Hachette UK Company
www.hachette.co.uk

www.piatkus.co.uk

SHEFFIELD HALLAM UNIVERSITY
WL
158.12
HA
COLLEGIATE LEARNING CENTRE

# INTRODUCTION

People often ask me "What is meditation like? How do you do it?" Let me answer these questions by using an example. It is spring in Perth as I write this book. It is the wettest season in twenty years, and the wildflowers are sensational. My "backyard" is Kings Park, which is 160 hectares of bushland between my home in Subiaco and the Swan River. I escape there at least once a day.

Often I enter the park with my head full of thoughts, mentally writing this book as I walk. But the scene is too lovely to ignore. The rainbow-coloured parrots are feeding on the bottlebrush flowers, the air is rich with scent, and the afternoon sun shines on the white bark of the gum trees.

Wildflowers are very seductive. Like babies and cats, they demand your attention. I soon find myself examining a blossoming bush. Some flowers are in full bloom, some are half-opened. Others are already drying out and decaying, but all are perfect. An ant is running up the stem, and the broken strands of a cobweb waft on the still air. The thoughts and concerns I brought into the park have all slipped away. I am in a different time and space.

This is meditation, a state in which the body is relaxed, the mind is quiet, and we are alive to the sensations of the moment.

We all know moments like these. They are everyday events. They happen to all of us when conditions are right — perhaps while stroking a cat, or listening to music, or enjoying a cup of tea on the veranda.

Yet when conditions are not right, we can walk through the park and be aware of nothing but our thoughts, worries and obsessions. Those peaceful moments don't always come easily. They most frequently occur when something holds our attention. At such times the mind is focused. It is not drifting aimlessly. Focusing the mind is the secret of meditation.

We meditate by focusing on something. This becomes our meditation object. Anything will do. However, people commonly meditate on breathing, a single repeated word, a flower or a mental image. We lightly examine it to help distance ourselves from thoughts.

This is easy to do for a few seconds. But the mind soon wants more entertainment, and starts thinking again. The challenge is to let the thoughts go and return to the object, again and again and again. Each time we drop a thought, the mind feels freer.

When we try to meditate, the world doesn't vanish and we don't pass into oblivion. Thoughts still arise, a headache may remain and noises may disturb us. Gradually they become less aggravating and we feel more at ease regardless.

Meditation is much more than a technique for relaxing. It also makes our minds more clear and alert. We become more sensitive to our own feelings and the detail of the world around us. We call this quality of mind "awareness". It is what distinguishes a meditator from someone who is simply relaxed.

If we meditate for a few minutes each day, the results can be deep and long-lasting. As we become more relaxed and aware, every aspect of our life can benefit. This book invites you to try it out and see.

For the last seven years, teaching meditation has been my full-time occupation. (This doesn't stop people from asking me "Do you have a real job as well?"). I teach between 150 and 200 people each term in eight-week-long courses at the Perth Meditation Centre, and run many workshops, seminars and retreats.

This book contains all the basic exercises and

explanations I give in class — as much as is possible in print, anyway. It contains all that you need to teach yourself. I have also tried to make the book clear enough so others can use it as a manual to teach from.

When I first learnt meditation, I often found the explanations I received difficult to understand. I would ask my teachers, "How does meditation work? What happens physically and mentally? What are the best techniques?" The usual reply was, "Do it and find out."

When I started to teach seven years ago, I tried to answer all those questions. I became the kind of teacher I wanted to meet twenty-five years ago. But this is not just a "how to" book. I also want you to know how and why meditation works, and what you are likely to discover along the way.

When we understand meditation, it becomes surprisingly simple — in principle at least. It is like finding the light switch after hours groping in the dark. People often meditate with little understanding of the process. Not surprisingly, they usually get mediocre results. It is like driving at night without headlights. The catch-phrase of this book is "Be aware! Know what you are doing."

This book is in three parts. Part Two is the meat in the sandwich, where all the important "how to" instructions are given. You can start right there, if you want to.

Chapter 1 explains how I teach, and how to use this book to teach yourself. Chapter 2 outlines why people meditate and the unexpected benefits they discover once they learn. Chapter 3, "What is Meditation?", answers the questions I am most frequently asked when I talk to the public. It outlines the basic principles of relaxing and focusing, different techniques, how to recognise deeper states of mind, and so on.

This book encourages you to listen to your body. If we are more aware of our physical stress, we can release it (Chapter 4); if we are more aware of the sensations of relaxation, we can enhance them (Chapter 5).

Part Two, Getting Started, is a self-contained, teach-yourself course in meditation. It contains the 10 core meditation practices that I have found work best for people. Each chapter presents a key idea, and is followed by a related exercise. Chapter 6, for example, explains the art of focusing, or paying attention, and is followed by the Breath meditation.

Getting Started explains all you need to meditate well. It is a ready-mix kit: just add time. If you invest 15 minutes a day, five days a week, for two months, you will be more relaxed, aware, healthier and in tune with yourself and the world. For a total of 10 hours' practice, you can learn a skill that may permanently benefit the rest of your life.

Sprinkled throughout the text are "spot meditations". You can do these whenever an opportunity presents itself — at traffic lights, in a supermarket queue, walking the dog. They take almost no time and can be very enjoyable. If you want to be relaxed right through the day, and not just when you formally meditate, try these exercises.

Part Three, Meditation in Daily Life, explains how to integrate meditation into our lives. Many people think of their meditation just as a few minutes of formal daily practice. However it can become a quality of mind that is with us continually. We can be calm and aware in any activity — even in emotionally charged situations! Part Three describes meditation as a tool for living well in this difficult, beautiful and unpredictable world of ours.

# PART ONE

# WHY MEDITATE?

# CHAPTER ONE

# GETTING THE MOST FROM THIS BOOK

The people with whom you learn meditation and the place you are taught it set a tone that is just as important as the instructions. The masseuse who works at the Perth Meditation Centre says she loves to hear the bursts of laughter and the lively discussion that often follow a meditation. Certainly there is nothing solemn about my classes. Even if students can't remember the instructions, they learn from the atmosphere.

There are many places you can learn to meditate. Even if the techniques were identical (which they are, in essence), the setting will shape your view of meditation. You may learn in a candle-lit room, with incense and dreamy music, reclining in chairs; or without any props, lying on the floor after a yoga class; or at an evening class at a local school, with the noise from the gymnasium next door; or in a place where men sit on the right and women on the left (no one explains why) and everyone sits on the floor.

Most of you will only have this book, and I can't transport you all to my classes in Perth. But it may help if you picture the way I teach, so you can put my words in context. This book closely follows the format of my beginners' classes. I hope something of their atmosphere comes through in the way I write.

Let us go back several years. When I came to Perth in 1986, I started teaching with a class of 12 people at a local learning centre. We could hear the shouts of the children at the creche, people gossiping at reception through the closed door, and various dramas proceeding up and down the corridors as we tried to meditate. This is what we call "meditation in daily life"!

I had already been meditating for 16 years. After my last seven-month retreat, my teacher encouraged me to teach, "but in your own way". This suited me because, although my training was Buddhist, I did not want to teach in that rather hierarchical format.

As any meditator knows, meditation is a practical skill with benefits that are obvious to anyone. It is a natural faculty of the human mind, not the property of any culture. I felt sure it could be explained in non-religious language, without throwing out the baby with the bathwater.

It seemed that Perth wanted a meditation teacher. My classes grew rapidly, and within a few months I was able to support myself solely from teaching. I have lived, breathed and slept meditation for seven years now. When I come home from a hard day's teaching, I give myself a break — and meditate!

Initially I taught at universities, schools, civic centres, government offices and from my home. The surroundings often left something to be desired. I was glad to leave them behind when I opened up the Perth Meditation Centre in West Perth.

The Centre is a top-floor office suite about as large as a suburban house. The main teaching room is large, symmetrical and airy with natural light coming through windows on three sides. It is carpeted and simply furnished in light colours with jungles of vegetation in the corners. Being on the top floor of a freestanding building with views of the sky, the room has the feeling of hanging in space.

If you were attending a class and came early, you may have a cup of tea in the reception room, or talk with other students. Or you may go into the teaching room, and relax in silence. When the class begins, up to 20 people will be sitting in a circle of chairs.

At your first class, you would find out who your companions are. On average, two or three would have cancer or some critical illness. Others want to meditate to help them through a life drama. Two or three may be students, hoping to improve their study. Professionally, about one third will be either nurses, doctors, physiotherapists, counsellors, administrators or teachers — in other words, people who work a lot with people. There are likely to be one or two creative artists, or keen sportspeople. Others are people who "need time to themselves" — especially mothers! There may be a few retired folk making good use of their leisure time. Their ages range from 15 to 70.

They come for every conceivable reason (Chapter 2 explains these in detail), yet all have to start at the same point: learning consciously to relax. They attend one class a week for eight weeks.

A typical class format would be: general discussion — long meditation — discussion — teabreak — shorter meditation — discussion. People often talk over personal matters with me before and after a class.

I teach through guided meditations. In other words, I keep people on track by talking them through the meditations. It is like helping someone learn to ride a bike.

You run alongside them, holding the carrier to keep them upright. As the course progresses, my instructions diminish, and they wobble off on their own.

In the first meditation, people may feel sleepy as they let themselves relax and their adrenalin levels drop. They often come to class after a hard day's work, and need to rest. But although they relax, I insist they stay awake, and I (almost!) always get my way. Meditation is not about going to sleep! The discussion afterwards helps people understand what happened in the session.

People are usually brighter in the second meditation, which is usually one aimed to develop clarity of mind, or introduce the kind of practices that can be done whenever an opportunity presents during the day. We may do just one exercise, or three or four in quick succession.

Over eight weeks, we cover all the exercises in Part 2, usually more than once, and from various angles. People soon recognise which practices suit them best, and work primarily with those. By sampling the whole range, even if they don't practise them all later, they understand the principles better.

It is easy to enter deep states of meditation in a class. People who are afraid they won't be able to need not worry. In a supportive environment, free from distractions and with the guidance of a teacher, meditation comes easily.

If people just want to see what meditation is like and understand it better, coming to a class is sufficient. However, to be able to meditate independently once the course is over requires practice.

On any day, read a chapter from Part Two and do the subsequent meditation. I suggest you try most of them over several days. Then work primarily with the one that appeals most. Spend a week or two with it, so the procedure becomes automatic. Make it your core practice, and then experiment with others.

Be patient and disciplined. You are most unlikely to do the exercise perfectly the first time you try. It takes repetition to retrain the responses in the body. Don't expect the same effects each day.

Amongst the text are the "spot meditations". These are mostly informal versions of the 10 basic meditations. They can be done anywhere the opportunity presents itself. The "red-light" meditation, at the end of this chapter, is one of these. They help dissolve stress and enhance relaxation through the day. Improvise with them. They can be fun.

Do you want to learn to meditate? If you read this book, do one 15-minute meditation a day, and three spot meditations a day, you can become a meditator in two months. That is only about 15 hours practice in all. If you can meet this challenge, the odds are 4 to 1 you will succeed.

Students who are happy with their progress often make the following comments:

*"It is much easier if I do it at the same time every day." (This is usually in the morning after waking, at night before bed, or just after they come home from work.)*

*"The spot-meditations are wonderful. I am doing lots of them. But I find they really only work well if I also do formal practice occasionally."*

*"I am not doing much formal practice, but I consciously look for ways to be more relaxed. I don't know if I am meditating but I feel much better."*

In Chapter 14 I describe how best to support your practice. You can attend groups, go on retreats, talk with meditators and teachers, and so on. This will only work if you have a practice there to support! If you are practising on your own, for 15 minutes a day, you will be 80 per cent of the way there.

# Spot meditation: RED LIGHT

This exercise works best if you are late, in a hurry — and the traffic lights turn red just as you approach.

## *Instructions*
If you feel frustrated, smile at yourself.
You have been given perhaps a whole minute to stop and do nothing.
Let body and mind slow down and relax.
Take a deep sigh, lingering on the out-breath.
Let your face and belly soften.
One whole minute to breathe softly.
Be aware of excess tension in your body.
Gently shake it free, as you settle back into the seat.
Look around you slowly.

The exercise finishes as the light turns green. Now devote all your attention to the task at hand: driving safely and well. And look forward to the next red light.

# CHAPTER TWO

# WHY DO PEOPLE MEDITATE?

I am always surprised when people ask me, "Why do you meditate?" It's like asking "Why do you breathe?" When my meditation practice is strong, I sleep well, rise early and the freshness of morning seems to last all day. I like people more and even the nuisances are tolerable. My thoughts are lucid, and I feel "on top of things".

The benefits of meditation ripple through everything we do. It is to have more energy, to be healthier, to think and work more efficiently and enjoy life more. Being relaxed and aware is the mental equivalent of being fit and healthy.

People often have a precise reason to meditate — to heal an illness or to study better, for example. They often get something different, or more than they expect. They come for relief from insomnia and find their relationships improve. They come for hypertension, and find peace and purpose in life. They may discover they are smoking or eating less, or that they don't need their glasses or asthma medication.

I often feel embarrassed talking about the benefits of meditation. Like those patent medicines of the last century, meditation seems to cure everything. I feel like a snake-oil salesman: "Meditation will help your insomnia, stomach cramps, poor memory, melancholy, PMT, and self-esteem. Oh yes, and your warts will disappear also!"

As a teacher, I don't need to sing the praises of meditation. In the class, people soon discover the benefits for themselves. This direct experience is worth a thousand words. They may have been thinking about meditation for years. Thirty minutes later, and they finally know what it feels like.

People often say to me "I hear meditation can cure cancer". I prefer to say that meditation supports a cure, rather than causes it. After all, even doctors don't "cure" anything. They only assist the natural healing processes of the body.

As support, meditation may be vital for healing. If we don't support a young tree, for example, it may blow over and die. But it would be only one of many factors in producing a healthy tree. Meditation may be the crucial factor that helps a person overcome cancer. But it is unlikely to be the sole cause. Lifestyle, diet and psychological factors would all play a part.

Wonderful as meditation is, I feel ashamed of the way some people promote it. Practising meditation is like building good health. It takes time and effort, and you should try to avoid having unrealistic expectations about what you can achieve. Yet some New Age advertisements depict it as a magical route to boundless wealth, sexual vigour, power over others and physical immortality. (I am not exaggerating!)

People meditate for many reasons:

Relaxation
Health
Inner peace and harmony
Concentration
To improve sporting or theatrical performance
Inspiration and creativity
Quality of life
Self-understanding and therapy
Spiritual awakening

In this chapter I will talk briefly about each of these.

# RELAXATION

After a serious crisis or years of chronic stress, many people lose their ability to relax. There are millions who require pills for a function as natural as sleeping. Being unable to relax can easily lead to a poor quality of life and health problems.

Learning to relax consciously, and to do it quickly, in any situation, is the first step in meditation. By relaxing, we unwind not just the body, but also the mental pre-occupations that wire us up in the first place.

Relaxing consciously is usually first done in a quiet place, with eyes closed. Eventually we can be relaxed while driving, eating, talking — even while having an argument. We don't blow the fuses, and can quickly repair ourselves at the end of the day.

# HEALTH

Just to be more relaxed each day is enormously valuable for our health. Meditation takes us one step further. Hundreds of medical surveys support the contention that meditation is good for health. These are the most common findings.

*Meditation releases muscular tension.* This automatically relieves pain, increases mobility and lets the body relax. The breath, the body fluids and the nerve impulses can flow more freely.

*Meditation lowers high blood pressure.* The release in muscular tension makes the body more pliable. The heart doesn't have to pump as hard to force the blood through the veins and arteries. When stressed, our blood becomes thick with cholesterol. This thins out when we relax.

*Meditation stimulates the immune system and the production of white blood cells.* The immune system winds down when the body is stressed. The healing process works best when the body is relaxed or sleeping. Meditation speeds recovery rates after illness or surgery.

*Meditation opens constricted air passages.* It is particularly good for asthmatics or hayfever sufferers.

*Meditation increases blood circulation to the digestive tract, the skin and the brain.* When we are stressed, our digestive system shuts down. The blood supply is redirected into the big muscles for the "fight-or-flight" reflex. Meditation reverses this, and the digestive system can function efficiently again.

The flow of blood to the skin and the extremities can be directly experienced as a pleasant tingling when you relax. Improved circulation means the entire body is better fed with nutrients and waste products removed more efficiently.

*Meditation dramatically affects hormonal activity.* This is a complex finding that still needs interpretation. Obviously, the stress hormones diminish during meditation. However it also appears that a meditator's pattern of hormonal secretions is generally typical of someone five or ten years younger than themselves. This suggests that the physical stresses of age do not weigh so heavily on a meditator. Meditators are like people who are very fit. They often look younger than their actual age.

*Meditation balances left and right hemisphere activity.* Each hemisphere of the brain governs the motor co-ordination of the opposite side of the body. If one hemisphere is overactive, the body can tend to be slightly lopsided, twisted or out of balance. This naturally creates physical tension. Anxious people tend to tie themselves in knots.

I use the presence of body imbalance as a diagnostic tool. I often take a mental snapshot of students when I first meet them. As the weeks progress I expect to see their general posture becoming more symmetrical as their hemispheric activity is balanced.

Simplistically, the left hemisphere usually governs thinking while the right governs feeling. Many of us get caught in one side or the other. We may be thinking excessively all day, or awash with emotion. Meditation balances these. A meditator is capable of clear thinking while still in tune with his or her emotional responses.

*General health indications.* The medical evidence suggests that meditation can be particularly effective with insomnia, migraines, asthma, chronic pain, hypertension, allergies and recovery after illness. It frequently has positive results with psychosomatic disorders of the skin, digestive tract and nervous system.

The anecdotal evidence indicates that meditation acts occasionally as a "magic bullet". Insomniacs and migraine sufferers are most likely to report quick and lasting results. Meditation can strip off the top 20 per cent of tension that triggers insomnia or a migraine attack.

In fact meditation generally acts like naturopathic treatment: it brings the whole body into harmony. The results are slower, more pervasive and not as easy to measure scientifically. However, we can assume meditation is useful for most ailments, not just those listed above. Most people, after three or four weeks of steady practice, will report improvement in general health and well-being.

# INNER PEACE AND HARMONY

We may feel that inner peace is impossible because the world or our life is in chaos. Yet tranquillity, however fleeting, is always with us when we relax. In those moments when we fully enjoy the beauty of nature or play with our dog, our fear and anger are suspended, whatever the day was like. Even chronic pain seems more tolerable.

# CONCENTRATION

Stress undermines our ability to concentrate. If we try to think and do a dozen different things at once, we do none of them well.

Meditation trains us to focus on one thing at a time. We become skilled at discarding the mental trivia and unproductive obsessions. This gives space for us to work, so we can bring all of the mind to the task at hand.

# TO IMPROVE PERFORMANCE

In the United States of America, many meditation teachers earn their living training sports people and stage performers. Such people realise meditation gives them the edge they need for peak performance. They know that operating solely at high adrenalin levels is counterproductive.

Great dancers, tennis players and actors have a grace and ease in performance. They are relaxed. They use just the right amount of energy for the task at hand. A hockey player told me "meditation is wonderful for me. We lost the grand final, but I played my best game of the season. I always had plenty of time to get where I was going. I could rest in the pauses. I felt the surges of energy going where they needed to in the body."

# INSPIRATION AND VISION

"I get so many ideas during a meditation class," said one visual artist, "They last all week." Meditation puts verbal thought in the background and creates a space for inspiration to arise. We can activate the right side of the brain and dream consciousness while fully awake. This promotes the flashes of insight that often emerge in daydream or reverie.

Meditation can help resolve difficult problems. It enables you to stand back, like withdrawing to a mountain to survey the terrain below. We can extract from the painful minutiae and get the big view. This process is not like "thinking things through". Answers often come in a flash when the mind is tranquil.

In the Buddhist tradition, inner wisdom (which is the only kind worth having) arises from these flashes of insight. They are moments when we can step aside from our ego-dramas and see things accurately. This is when the lights go on. The insights may just be "that cheese gives me a headache" or "I really don't like my wife", or we may have profound intuitions into issues facing us or philosophic questions.

# QUALITY OF LIFE

Monks and nuns are assumed to lead lives of deprivation: no sex, no entertainment, and eating restrictions. In fact, they may be leading lives of refined sensuality. Similarly, meditators can live in a world rich in sensing and feeling. To enjoy a simple meal with awareness is more satisfying than devouring a banquet with our minds elsewhere.

People often say to me "If I miss my morning sitting, the whole day becomes ragged." Beginners realise how valuable meditation is when they stop doing it for a while.

# SELF-AWARENESS AND THERAPY

Self-knowledge starts with an awareness of the body. The hallmark of neurosis is lack of this awareness. Such people don't even notice when they light another cigarette or put food in their mouths. They tend to live in their heads. Anorexics, for example, are obsessed with the idea, not the reality, of their bodies.

Meditation brings us down to earth. It puts us in touch with the sensations of our bodies. Recognising the reality of who we are may be uncomfortable, but self-awareness has to start with this. Relaxation loosens the tensions of the day. Deep relaxation can release the chronic in-built tension of years. This may in turn loosen the repressed emotions that set those tensions in place. When the mind is strong and tranquil, it often throws up buried memories and emotions, allowing them to be acknowledged and cleared. In its own way, meditation covers exactly the same ground as any psychotherapy.

# SPIRITUAL AWAKENING

For the spiritual path we need to clear the mind and listen. The Christian mystic, Meister Ekhardt, said we must become a space for God to enter into. The Buddhist tradition says the same: only the empty bowl can receive wisdom. We can't think our way to God: grace can come only when the mind is open and receptive.

Our minds are often polluted by an endless parade of trivial thoughts and fantasies. Meditation can weed these out as they arise from moment to moment. The Buddhist tradition says "When you master the small moments, the great moment is at hand."

It may seem that a person aiming for spiritual awakening will meditate differently from someone trying to overcome insomnia, yet the ground rules are the same for both. To succeed, both people need to be relaxed and aware in meditation and in daily life.

Anything we do with our minds, we do better if we meditate. Meditation is like learning to drive a car. There are certain inescapable procedures we have to follow. But once we learn, it is up to us where we drive.

# CHAPTER THREE

# WHAT IS MEDITATION?

**W**hat is meditation? How does it work? In this chapter, I give an outline of the main ideas that will be explained more fully in the rest of the book.

## MEDITATION: THE ART OF BEING RELAXED AND ALERT

A question I often face is "What is the difference between relaxation and meditation?" People rightly suspect that meditation is more than just being relaxed.

Meditation is a calm and alert state of mind. It is when the body is relaxed and the mind is focused. It is when thoughts drop aside, and we are at one with the sensations of the moment.

Relaxation, on the other hand, is when the mind wanders. It may drift between sleep and fantasy and thought. We may be only half-awake and may not even know what we are thinking. It is a pleasant state but out of control.

We are most likely to be relaxed and alert when we are focused on something we enjoy. It may be while we are:

* listening to music
* watching the birds in the backyard
* doing yoga, or any exercise with awareness
* having a shower
* eating a peach
* arranging flowers
* lying in bed, listening to the wind and the rain

One woman told me: "When my kids were little, I would lie on the couch in the afternoon to rest. My eyes were closed and my body felt asleep, but I was quite awake. I kept track of the kids by listening to the sounds they made." She was relaxed but her mind was alert.

We can also be relaxed and alert sitting in a chair, feeling our body gently expand and contract as we breathe. This is actually meditating on the breath.

Meditation is a balancing act: we may be relaxed but not very awake; or we may be alert but physically tight. Sometimes we need to relax more; at other times we need to brighten up. Usually we are too alert: our anxieties keep us wired-up. With fine-tuning and practice, we can achieve the best of both worlds.

Early in a course, students often err on the side of drowsiness. I am happy about this. They have to reach square one at least. It is easier to wake up a relaxed mind than to calm down an over-alert one. For some people, it is quite an achievement to be nodding off in a chair in a roomful of people! By the final weeks, however, they should be mentally sharp as their bodies relax.

# FOCUSING AND THE BASIC INSTRUCTIONS

We keep the mind alert as we relax by focusing on something. This helps keep us awake and holds any distracting thoughts at bay.

The basic instructions for most meditations are the same:

1. Relax
2. Choose one thing to focus on and explore
3. If the mind wanders, bring it back
4. Let everything else go

In other words, we give the mind a simple task to keep it out of trouble. We might, for example, count the breaths or say a mantra. This is our anchor. When our attention strays, we pull ourselves back to it.

It may sound like work, and indeed it is. We love to play with our thoughts – chasing the good ones, battling with the bad. We don't want to give up our worries and fantasies, however frustrating they may be. Yet clearly we have to let go this mental dogfight if we want to relax. Letting go can be hard work!

Focusing, or concentration, is the basic technique of almost every meditation. The term can be problematic for some people, who associate it with knitted brows and grim determination. For this reason, some teachers claim their practices do not involve focusing. But they do. I explain the term more fully in Chapter 6.

Good focusing is joyful. It is like a child fascinated with a toy — sensing and feeling, not thinking. We are focused when all other thoughts and sensations are momentarily backstage or dimmed out. Focusing happens naturally, as in the examples given at the beginning of this chapter, but it is also a skill we can develop.

# DIFFERENT PRACTICES AND THEIR EFFECTS

There are thousands of different meditations. Yet the instructions for most of them are similar: relax, focus on one object or activity, and let all else drop aside. The main difference between the different meditations is the object on which we choose to focus.

The most widely used meditations are:

1. Breath and body awareness
2. Mantra and affirmations
3. Visualisation
4. Sense objects (nature, music, candle, sound, etc.)

There are countless variations on these. And this is just the beginning. Eventually we can meditate on memories, a problem, pain, emotions, abstract principles, God, or on the nature of the mind itself. But it is best to start on something simpler. We learn to walk before we run.

I am often asked "Which is the best meditation?" This is like asking which medicine is best. Medicine only has value if it suits the person who uses it. This explains why there is such a choice of meditations. If you try out a variety, you will soon know whether a practice is right or wrong for you. It will be obvious: either you like it or you don't. Be like a dog sniffing something on the street: trust your instinct; if it smells good, eat it.

Most meditations have a similar goal: to enhance our ability to relax and focus. Given that, however, different practices do have different effects. It is useful to know of these.

Breath- and body-based meditations tend to foster self-awareness, health, memory, relaxation and bliss. They are good, all-round practices, which can, however, lead to excessive self-analysis (see Chapters 6, 7 and 10).

Mantra and affirmations are ideal to promote tranquillity. They are simple and flexible to do, suit people of a religious or devotional temperament, and often produce joy at the expense of clarity of mind (see Chapter 9).

Visualisations are positive, creative and individualistic. They can tap the potential of the mind, yet often lack depth. They can lead to a greedy state of mind that wants results — visions and insight — from each meditation (see Chapter 12).

Sense-object meditations take you out of yourself and enhance your empathy with, and understanding of, the outer world (see Chapter 11).

Many people usually find that breath and bodyscan meditations are the most useful foundation practices. But other meditations — music, mantra and affirmations — are easier, so you may prefer to start with those.

Many groups have strong preferences about meditation techniques. Southern Buddhists tend to prefer the breath; Hindu groups like mantra. New Agers like visualisation and affirmations, and so on. Each group tends only to teach their favoured practice.

This is rather crude. It is like deciding that everyone

needs more Vitamin C or zinc in their diet. Newcomers often feel like failures if they don't take to the given practice. It is more likely that the technique didn't suit their temperament. Meditation is a very individual path. Everyone can meditate if they find a suitable means.

# POSTURE

We can meditate in any posture — sitting, standing, walking or lying down — and anything in between (see Chapter 7). Each posture has a different mental effect and no particular posture is "best". It is not our posture but how we hold ourselves in it that matters.

Find out which chair or combination of cushions suits you best. You need to be comfortable (but not too comfortable). Your posture should be open enough for you to breathe easily (no slumping shoulders). And there should be a gentle alertness in your posture (meditating in bed has its dangers!).

# ALPHA AND BETA BRAINWAVES

When we relax, our minds literally slow down. You can tell: your mind doesn't jump from thought to thought so rapidly. It is convenient to call this state "alpha", since the alpha brainwaves (between 7 and 14 cycles per second) are dominant when we relax. The faster brainwaves (14 to 30 c.p.s.) are called "beta". This is our usual mentally active state of mind. Sleep brainwaves are called theta and delta.

The alpha state has a distinct mental quality we can learn to cultivate. In alpha, sensing is predominant to thinking. We are mentally receptive rather than active. Our attention is in the present rather than in the past or future.

Alpha is an accepting and non-judgemental state. (More about alpha and beta states in Chapter 8.)

# RECOGNISING DEEPER STATES OF MIND

Meditation expands the boundaries of consciousness. We start to become familiar with the outskirts of conscious-ness — particularly the states closer to sleep. Classically, this progression is described as:

1. Being aware while awake
2. Being aware while relaxed
3. Being aware in the dream state
4. Being aware in dreamless sleep

We may notice that as our metabolism slows down, our state of mind also changes. In beta, our usual waking state, the mind is like a grasshopper as we are constantly think-ing, talking, mentally active and "on stage". Our body feels solid or tense, and our softer feelings are kept in the wings.

When we are relaxed and in alpha, the activity of the mind feels slower. The mind drifts, sees images or colours, or fantasises. We experience the body directly as sen-sations that come and go: aches and pains, soft tingling feelings, and so on.

When closer to sleep, the mind becomes "irrational". Dream images or old memories may flit by. Unexpected insights ("that's where I left the car keys!") may pop up. The concerns of the day slip away. The body feels heavy or light, or floaty, or may seem to vanish completely. The body feels quite different from the way it feels in the beta state.

As we approach this "body asleep, mind awake" state, it becomes harder to stay alert. This is not surprising since we have had decades of conditioning to drop off to sleep at this point. To stay awake means breaking an ingrained habit. We also have to be convinced it is worth doing.

At what point do you lose consciousness? Some people drift off in the very first stages of alpha. However if we can stay awake as the body approaches sleep, the rewards are infinitely richer.

Have you ever woken from a sleep feeling miraculously alive and bright? You know you had a wonderful sleep, though you remember nothing of it. Some part of you knew. The "body asleep, mind awake" state in meditation is like this.

It is healthy to be more relaxed in everyday life. However, profound healing is more likely to occur in the "body asleep, mind awake" state. The chronic anxieties that hound us, whether awake or asleep, are not present in this state. The psychological causes of ill health are cut off at the root. The self-healing mechanism of the whole psyche moves into action, for those moments at least (see Chapters 10 and 17).

# BEING RELAXED AND AWARE DURING THE DAY

There are deeper states than those outlined above, which are hard enough to describe, let alone experience. Much more important is to develop breadth in your practice — to be centred and aware right through the day.

I don't give my students pass or fail marks. Nonetheless, I look to see if they can pass two critical thresholds. Can the student stay alert while deeply relaxed? It takes a while to become strong and centred in this state. Unfortunately I meet some people who spend years "meditating" without getting this far.

The next threshold is to be consciously relaxed and aware through the day, outside the formal meditation session. It is easy to relax in a class, lying down, with your eyes closed, someone guiding you, a quiet atmosphere and the support of other meditators. Gradually you need to abandon these props so you can meditate sitting up or walking, with eyes open, no one guiding you, in noisy circumstances and in the company of people who think you are a fool.

It may take a few attempts, but you can soon learn to meditate with your eyes open. This gives great flexibility and extra clarity of mind. You can meditate at waiting rooms, while walking, at lectures. You can meditate on things of beauty – the sky, the ocean, a bush in flower, birds in flight. You can meditate in the midst of activity. You can learn to meditate in different postures, no longer needing a certain chair or cushion or room. You are able to meditate at the dentist or waiting to pick up the kids from school.

Eventually you can meditate when circumstances are far from ideal – when you can hear the TV next door, and the traffic outside, and the kids fighting down the hall. You may be exhausted, angry or miserable, yet you find meditation is not only possible: it is just what you need. At this point our meditation starts to become a continuous practice. It is the art of always finding the point of balance in the unpredictable weather of our lives.

## GOING FOR THE BLISS

Many meditators are "bliss-junkies." They just want the "good" meditations. They may become addicted to the props – the people, the setting, the method, and often the philosophy behind it. This can unfortunately make their meditation dependent on a place, a time of day, a certain emotional state. If any of these are less than ideal, the meditation doesn't feel right.

You can become entangled in a plethora of "dos and don'ts" if you are just chasing the ultimate high: don't meditate after a meal; eat vegetarian food only; sit in lotus, cross-legged on the floor; wear white or black; learn how to breathe "correctly"; sit like a statue; use only this mantra; don't tamper with other methods; have only pure and noble thoughts; abandon things that hinder your spiritual growth such as work, family, culture; and so on.

These systems are valuable but they are not necessary if you are looking for awareness and balance in your life. Meditation doesn't require us to withdraw from reality. Rather it is a habit of being relaxed and in tune with ourselves physically and emotionally through the day. This continuous inner balance is more valuable than the occasional "high".

# Spot meditation:
# RANDOM OBJECT

This technique can be practised during any free moment, for example sitting at your desk, or waiting at a bus stop or in your car.

## Instructions
Pick out an interesting object in your field of vision. It could be an acacia flower, the grass swaying in the wind, a pattern on someone's shirt

Settle your mind there. Drop the inner talk. Shift into sensing.

Let your eyes soften a little (don't stare).

Use your eyes like a zoom lens. Let time slow down and explore the object at your leisure. Imagine its texture or smell, if appropriate. Allow associations to arise.

Let your body soften and relax.

Take a deep breath and sigh as you breathe out.

Be aware of the object, your body and the stream of attention linking them.

Finally, let the object go, consciously.

Check how your mindstate has changed.

Are you more calm and aware?

# CHAPTER FOUR

# BEING AWARE OF STRESS

S tress is not an external force beyond our control because it occurs within our bodies. It is usually an excessive fear or anger response, with its own cocktail of hormones, gearing the body for fight-or-flight. Unfortunately, our attention is usually directed outwards at the apparent problem, rather than inwards at our reactions to it.

We usually try to ignore stress rather than face it. Stress is uncomfortable, but it is easy to block out temporarily. We can talk, eat, drink, work, watch TV, or take a pill. But the monster doesn't vanish because we cover our eyes with our hands. A pain-killer is not a cure.

If there is a magic bullet for stress, it is to become more self-aware. The simplest way to relieve stress is to sense it, in detail, in the body. If we can feel it dispassionately, without our usual fear and anxiety, the stress will start to loosen, almost of its own accord. We don't have to "do" anything, it just happens. But if we try to block stress out, it can remain literally for years.

Shall we do a simple exercise to illustrate this? Don't change your posture, or put this book aside. Close your eyes, and slowly scan your body. You probably thought you were relaxed. But as you sense yourself in detail, you are likely to find areas of excess tension. These are parts of the body that are more tense than they need to be for the task of simply reading a book. You may be twisted awkwardly, one shoulder may be tight, your jaw may be clenched or the breathing cramped. Try it out and see!

Do you also see how a point of tension releases, almost automatically, as soon as you notice it? The jaw drops a little, the shoulder softens. We do it instinctively. We can increase that effect by wriggling a little. Notice how easy it is to relieve tension when you know exactly where it is. Consider how long it would have remained if you hadn't noticed it.

Of course, the pain may still be there. The important question is "Is there improvement?" The tension may be 10 per cent or 20 per cent less. It may seem easier to block the pain with our usual strategies. However the cure is to allow discomforts to surface in your consciousness and allow them to release, little by little.

We dial the phone with a knot in our stomach. We sit hunched at our desks, unwilling to breathe. We drive with a stranglehold on the steering wheel. We read a book with clenched jaw and furrowed brow. This is excess tension and is more than we need for the task at hand. It is useless effort. We actually do the job less effectively. Yet we can release this strain as soon as we notice it.

# THE PHYSICAL EFFECTS OF STRESS

Our response to stress often overshoots the mark. We may, for example, react to a snide comment as if we were physically attacked. In fact, many of our ailments – hypertension, allergies and so on – are our body's overreaction to a perceived threat. We are like certain third world countries – more at risk from our own defence forces than the enemy outside.

Extreme (or chronic) stress galvanises the body for action. Adrenalin and thyroid hormones speed the metabolism. The heart beats faster, we breathe more rapidly. Sugar, insulin and cholesterol are released into the bloodstream. The digestive and immune systems shut down. Cortisone and endorphins, the body's pain-killers, are released. The senses are heightened.

These prepare us for physical action. If we can act, they clear; if not, we burn out. The most natural release of stress is to use the muscles of the body (not the head!). It is, after all, the fight-or-flight mechanism. Our bodies are calling out to run, play squash, dig a garden or do aerobics. Or hit someone. The problem comes when we can't act physically.

After escaping a wild animal, we would relax naturally. Most of our dangers nowadays are more obscure and chronic. We can't run from the boss, the alcoholic relative, the recession or the ozone hole. The stress hormones gear us for action, but what can we do, physically? The fight-or-flight juices still surge through us, but with nowhere to go they poison us in time. They damage the arteries and the immune system, and predispose us to serious illness.

Some stress hormones make us numb. Soldiers in battle or people in brawls typically don't feel their injuries until later when they relax. If you suspect you are suffering from stress, you can assume the damage is worse than you think.

When powering through the day, we hardly notice, and often wilfully ignore, the signs that the engine is over-heating: headaches, indigestion, strain in the face. Eventually the body shouts at us. For many, the first danger sign they acknowledge will be the last: a heart attack.

# WHY PEOPLE ARE RELUCTANT TO RELAX

Do you actually want to relax? This may seem a silly question, but people are very ambivalent about relaxing. Operating on high adrenalin has its pay-off, and we like it. Conversely, relaxing often feels like a downer. Let us look at the many reasons why people are unwilling to relax.

If we relax, how would we get everything done? There is no doubt that people can achieve great things in their careers, for example, by operating on dangerously high stress levels. Rather than wind down, we may prefer to distract ourselves with something stimulating. We keep squeezing the adrenal glands, just in case. We want to relax while keeping the revs up, without taking the armour off. Stress can be a way of life. Many people feel they need a sparkling personality for work or home, but when you relax, the mask drops. It may feel most awkward just being yourself in the wrong company. If you came to work, acting as tired as you actually felt, what would people think of you?

Staying "tight" is a way of blocking our inner feelings. I remember a nun who walked out of one of my retreats. "If I relax", she said, "negative emotions come up." These feelings may have been stronger than she could cope with.

Blocking feelings may be a good short-term strategy. If

you are under pressure, say, during an illness or marriage break-up, it may not be useful to allow your true feelings to surface. It may be more important to hold yourself together and just get through. Relaxing too much could even be dangerous. The stress hormones, after all, are like armour. They help you go into battle.

We can be chemically addicted to stress. Cortisone and endorphins are pain killers, like morphine, and adrenalin acts like an amphetamine. People get hooked on stress; it is our own legal drug factory. We get a drug "high" when stressed. It is like a bribe or reward that keeps us going when sanity would have us stop.

Alcoholics and drug takers often feel powerful and in control of their destiny when they are "high". Stress can give the same effect. There is a pay-off to being Super-mum, even if you feel shattered by bedtime. Conversely you may feel awful and "not yourself", if you relax and go into withdrawal.

# WINDING DOWN FROM STRESS

Relaxing can be quite uncomfortable after extreme stress. If you had been involved in an accident, for example, the stress hormones would have enabled you to cope. You may walk away feeling good, but the after-effects may be nausea, vomiting, weakness, shivering, an aching body. You may be emotionally shaky for days. This is how nature rebalances the system.

As we relax, we come off the self-generated pain-killers and stimulants: we feel the truth inside us without a chemical filter. Relaxing can be like convalescence: a healthy process but often uncomfortable, both physically and emotionally. It is like being in hospital — lots of doing nothing and waiting.

We relax best if we don't fight the process. Our back or neck pain may seem like a huge, solid lump. But it developed through thousands of tiny moments of over-reaction and won't disappear in a flash. Relaxation is the reverse process. It happens in hundreds of tiny stage-by-stage loosenings.

Relaxation is like calming an upset child — a slow gradual process. If you hit your child and tell it to "stop whingeing", it won't calm down at all. We tend to have the same response towards stress: we want to "get rid of it" as if it is a loathsome parasite. But in reality it *is* us, so it is better to start a sensible dialogue with it.

We are stressed because we don't listen to our bodies. Often all we need to do is pay a little attention to them. With acceptance and awareness, the pain will start to loosen — but in its own time and pace. It doesn't help to be pushy. Trying to "make yourself relax" or "get rid of" the pain is often counter-productive.

Yet when we do simply watch, wait and accept, the relaxation process can be very swift. People often come to a class after work, stressed to the hilt. Their movements are rigid, their breathing is tight and they talk with animation to escape the emotional strain so obvious in their faces. Without meditation, they may still be revved-up when they try to sleep hours later.

In a class setting, however, they can relax to the edge of sleep in about six minutes, on average. I watch them as I guide them into meditation. At first, they sit rigid in the chair — or fidget endlessly. Gradually they make contact with their aches and pains, which can be many. At a certain point, the body loosens with an involuntary sigh. Eventually the fine muscles of the face soften visibly. I know they have arrived; the process is under way.

# Spot meditation: FREEZE

It is easy to crank up the tension during the day. But we rarely give ourselves time to relax. This meditation is designed to wind us down just a little: to strip off the top 20 per cent of tension. We don't need to function on peak adrenalin all day. Occasional moments of rest make us more efficient overall.

## *Instructions*

Tell yourself to "freeze".

Hold your posture, but not your breath.

You may be at your desk, doing the dishes or standing in a queue.

Scan your body slowly up and down, observing areas of excess tension.

Don't change anything yet.

Notice how you are breathing.

When you feel in tune with yourself, say "defrost".

Allow tension to release.

Make little adjustments wherever appropriate — sit or stand straighter, loosen shoulders, neck, eyes, stomach, hands.

Don't stop. Be systematic.

Enjoy making finer and finer adjustments.

Take a deep breath and sigh as you breathe out.

Feel yourself breathing.

Can you give the breath more space and freedom?

Notice how much your mood is changing.

Resume your former activity when ready, retaining an awareness of the body.

# CHAPTER FIVE

# WHY CAN'T WE RELAX?

**S**tress, like pain, can be a good friend. It tells us when our way of living is dangerous to our health. We usually don't want to hear this message, so we try to shut it out. This almost seems to work, except that the messenger makes quite a noise battering on the door, so not surprisingly, we often get the message wrong.

Strange to say, we are also unfamiliar with relaxation. We are usually not very perceptive when we relax. Our minds wander amid pleasant thoughts and fantasies. We mentally disconnect and drift towards sleep. Nothing seems to matter. We may say things like "I don't know what I was thinking about".

So we have trouble trying to relax because we don't know what to aim for. Many people can only think of relaxation as the absence of pain — a kind of oblivion. This is a difficult target. Relaxation is a much more positive state. If we know in detail what it feels like, then we can reach it more quickly. And if we are mentally alert, rather than lost in the clouds, we relax more profoundly.

I start my meditation courses by coaxing people into deep relaxation, while keeping them awake. I call this the "body asleep, mind awake" state. I ask that they become intimately aware of how their bodies feel when they relax.

Most people do this exercise sitting in chairs. Others get blankets and cushions to lie on the floor. For 20 or 30 minutes, I talk them into the "body asleep, mind awake" state. Although sleep is seductive, I make sure they stay awake. Again and again, I ask them to notice "what does relaxation actually feel like?" so they find their personal landmarks.

After the session, we discuss what people noticed. It is quite new for people to examine relaxation in such detail and they are often quite surprised by their body sensations. We all relax at least once each day, when we sleep. And yet for many, it is like the dark side of the moon: unexplored territory.

During the exercise, I cue people to observe features such as their breathing, feelings of heaviness or lightness, sensations on the skin, their heartbeat, perception of time, and quality of mind. Although people are idiosyncratic in their responses, there are common features most people can notice.

## STARTING TO RELAX

*"I didn't realise how tense I was."*

*"I was irritated by all the noises in the room, and it took me a long time to settle."*

As we relax, the hormonal painkillers fade, and the aches and pains of the day surface. We may find sore spots emerging everywhere — eyes, neck, head, stomach. Welcome these sensations because they are positive signs of the chemical shift from tension to relaxation.

As we relax we often become more aware of our surroundings. If we are tense, these often irritate us. However this indicates that the mind is shifting from a beta to an alpha state, from thinking to sensing.

## HEAVINESS OR LIGHTNESS

*"My body felt like lead."*

*"I seemed to fuse into the chair."*

*"I felt I was sinking deeper and deeper into myself."*

*"I felt heavy, but also as if I was floating just above the floor."*

*"My body felt huge, as if it filled the room."*

*"I couldn't feel my fingers (arms, legs, body). I wiggled them to make sure they were still there."*

Adrenalin "lifts" the body. As that fades away, the body seems to drop and become heavy. It surrenders to the floor or chair. Your hands may seem glued together.

After a period of heaviness, the feeling may shift. Your body may feel light, or empty, or floating. This is often how we feel just before we fall asleep. These feelings can be very clear if we focus on them and they are excellent indicators of our shift into a relaxed state.

## BREATHING

*"My breathing became very light, and often stopped for quite long periods."*

*"My breathing went right down into my belly."*

*"My breathing felt erratic and slow, but quite comfortable."*

*"I wondered if I should be breathing more."*

When we are tense, we usually breathe from the upper chest, and tend to hold our breath in. When we relax, however, we let the out-breath go completely. The whole belly loosens up. We also breathe less and there may be long unforced pauses at the end of the out-breath. As our metabolic rate drops we need less air. It takes a lot of oxygen to burn the energy needed to maintain physical tensions. As those tensions go, we don't need as much air. (More about breathing in Chapter 7.)

# SKIN SENSATIONS AND THE HEARTBEAT

*"My skin felt warm and tingly (or itchy)."*

*"I felt pleasantly warm all over, as if I was sitting in the sun. It stopped when the meditation finished."*

*"I could feel the heartbeat pulsing in my hands (belly, face)."*

*"My heartbeat sounded very loud."*

When you are tense, your blood is re-routed from your skin to the big inner muscles in preparation for fight-or-flight. The reverse happens when you relax. Blood flows back to the skin, making it warm and tingly, especially in the hands and face. The same process loosens congestion in the muscles. These may feel less rigid, or more soft and tingly. A good meditator may actually feel the blood moving in surges in the skin, like waves on the shore. Some people, usually about half the class, can also feel their hearts pulsing through their bodies. When we are tense, we rarely notice these subtle sensations.

## OTHER COMMENTS

*"I had a lot of saliva, and had to swallow frequently."*
  *"I couldn't stop my stomach gurgling."*
  *"My eyes watered."*

The digestive system shuts down when we are tense, and comes to life when we relax. Stomachs often gurgle in a class, much to people's embarrassment, and salivation may occur. Your eyes may water, too.

## MENTAL SIGNS

*"I saw swirling colours (dream images, memories)."*
  *"Time seemed to slow down. It felt like I hadn't breathed for minutes."*
  *"I was floating in this beautiful crystal-clear space."*
  *The sensations in my body (or sounds) were magnified to the nth degree."*

There are many mental indicators of relaxation like those described above. I will discuss these in more detail later.

People often wonder "Am I doing the meditation right?" If they can tune into their bodies, they will know. Are the physical signs there — heaviness or lightness, tingling on the skin, soft light breathing and so on? Does the body feel asleep, and the mind awake? As meditation becomes more profound, the body is the simplest yardstick to tell you what stage you have reached.

Quite simply we can say, when we are tense, our bodies

feel tight, hard and blocked. When we are relaxed, our bodies feel loose, soft and flowing. The breath flows, the juices within you flow, and there is a delicate inner movement as the body seeks to restore harmony and health.

Relaxation feels good. It feels healthy. Extensive medical research indicates that meditation releases muscular tension, increases circulation, lowers high blood pressure and so on. With practice, you actually feel these and many other changes within you. You meditate because you can feel it working. It ceases to be something you do "because my doctor told me to".

It should be obvious now, what meditation is not. It is not a state of oblivion. Neither are you a stone buddha. In meditation, the body feels alive, fluid and healthy like that of a sleeping baby. The mind is awake and perceptive.

Some people are apprehensive at the first class. "I've always been uptight. My doctor told me to come here, but I don't think I'll ever relax." Yet after two or three weeks, they know the feeling in their own flesh and blood.

They have made the first step, but the next one is larger. Relaxation is not just a slow-metabolic state close to sleep. We can also be relaxed right through the day.

When I speak of being relaxed while walking, some wit in the class usually makes facetious comments about blundering into trees. But we can be relaxed or tense during any activity. We are relaxed when we use just the right amount of energy for the activity we are engaged in. It is when our energy output is just right — not too much, not too little. We don't have to be slow and quiet to be relaxed. We can walk, talk, work, eat or play sport being either relaxed or unnecessarily tense. A great dancer or gymnast or football player in action is graceful and easy, with no excess tension.

If we watch people walking through the city streets, it

is obvious who is relaxed and who is tense. You can almost feel the stiff legs, the knotted stomachs, the anguish in the shoulders. Some people are burning enough energy to drive a bus.

For a few days you might like to observe yourself getting dressed in the morning. Notice how you take a shirt off its hanger. Are your movements comfortable and flowing or are they frantic and jerky? Are you tense? Burning more energy than necessary? Or moving harmoniously?

We may not think that the way we get dressed contributes to our stress. But thousands of moments of excess tension during the day take their toll as much as one big event. Paying attention to these helps the tension diminish.

Relaxation may seem like some exotic practice you have to go to a professional to learn. But the secret is that it starts right here: in the way you answer the telephone, the way you drive your car. And all it takes is awareness (perhaps a little more than usual!).

## Spot meditation: SLOWING DOWN

This exercise helps you notice the speed at which you are moving. When you are tense, this is often faster and more spasmodic than necessary. This exercise helps you turn down your metabolic rate. The basic instruction is simple. For a few minutes, consciously do everything the slightest fraction slower.

### Instructions

Choose a simple activity you do every day. It could be:

- getting dressed
- having a shower

- leaving the house and getting into the car
- having breakfast, or a teabreak
- watering the plants
- taking the dog for a walk

Make the activity into a spot meditation. Give it a start and finish. Allow an extra minute or two, so you don't have to hurry. Do every movement just the slightest fraction slower. Notice the pace at which you walk, turn, sit, lift things. Otherwise, be natural.

Notice when you are hurried and jerky, when you are smooth and easy. Are you breathing easily? Or holding your breath?

Consciously enjoy the passing sensations — the water on your face, the taste of toast, the texture of your shirt, the click as you turn the key in the lock.

Keep the mind here and now. When you disappear into thought, come back to the sensations of the present.

When you finish, be still for ten seconds and notice how you feel. Practise the same activity for four days, and see how it changes.

PART TWO

# GETTING STARTED

# CHAPTER SIX

# FOCUSING

T he basic instructions for most meditations are the same:

1. Relax
2. Choose one thing to focus on and explore it
3. If the mind wanders, bring it back
4. Let all else go

The basic difference between meditations is the object we choose to focus on. In the following chapters, we will meditate on the breath, the body (in two different ways), music, affirmations, mantra, a visualisation, and a visual object. In addition, there are two meditations, "clearing" and "naming", which seem to bend the guidelines above.

# THE BASIC TECHNIQUE — FOCUSING

Focusing occurs naturally when something interests us or catches our attention. We are focused when we are thinking of nothing else. You are focusing when you: enjoy the texture and colour of a silk scarf, are engrossed in a good book, savour the first mouthful of a good soup, carefully apply eye make-up, or clean the car window at the petrol station.

When one of these activities is in the foreground of our mind, other thoughts slip into the background. But as soon as our attention disengages from the scarf or the soup, the other thoughts surface again instantly. This is how focusing performs that minor miracle: stopping thoughts (or should we say, gently nudging them aside).

The key to good focusing is to be interested in the object or activity. Of course, the breath may not be as interesting as the first taste of a fine soup. But if we can approach it with the same gentle curiosity, it becomes so.

So we try to become interested in the shifting moment-to-moment detail of the breath. It is a succession of muscular sensations, ripples and flows, that come and go within us. We may feel it most clearly in the belly or the chest or the nostrils. We notice when it stops and starts, or how smooth or jerky it feels. We don't try to change it. We don't "think about" it. We just feel it as it is happening.

As we focus the mind slows down. We become attentive and relaxed, and other thoughts slip away. Of course it is not that easy. After focusing on our breathing for a few seconds, we find some thought of burning importance calls us away ("Shall I iron that shirt now or tomorrow? I wonder what's on TV tonight?"). The breath seems boring in comparison.

This, therefore, is the spadework in meditation: drop

the thought and return to the object of focus. Meditation works on the deferred pleasure principle. If we can drop the cheap satisfaction of thoughts and fantasy, the rewards are so much greater. Each time we drop a thought, we enjoy a moment of liberation. Gradually the mind becomes bright and clear, and capable of insight.

To meditate we choose an object — the breathing, a flower, a mantra or an image — and put a "fence" around it. Buddhist texts call the meditation object the "workplace". Our work is to stay within the fence and explore.

Like any workman, we are aware of things beyond the fence, but we don't have to down tools and pursue them. Sounds easy, doesn't it? But before we know it, some seductive thought strolls by and we're halfway down the road after it.

Good concentration is very gentle, almost effortless. The essence of focus is actually to let go. The mind will naturally focus if we can quickly disengage from other thoughts.

But this is the ideal. The reality is very different. Our thoughts are like mobs of schoolchildren clamouring for a teacher's attention. By focusing on something, you can say to them: "I'm busy now, come back later". And just like children, some thoughts are most reluctant to go, some go and come back later, while some never come back at all.

Focusing *doesn't* mean blocking out every other thought. This is an impossibility anyway. Instead it is more like operating a camera lens: when we focus on a nearby flower with our camera, it comes into sharp focus. The background is still there, but a little fuzzy. Similarly, when we are centred on the breath, other thoughts and sensations still arise, but on the periphery.

Some people assume that to be aware of anything, you must automatically be "thinking about it". But are you "thinking about" your cat as you stroke its back and tweak its ears? Focusing is non-verbal, sensuous and immediate: it involves sensing not thinking.

# DISTRACTIONS AND THE WANDERING MIND

Yet there seem to be so many distractions. A door slams nearby. A painful thought or great idea arises. What do we do? We allow ourselves to feel it for a moment, then drop it and go back to the breath. It takes a while to realise we don't need to dwell on everything that arises in our minds.

A slamming door and its reverberation in your body lasts only a second. The real distraction will be how you react to it. What do you do? Get annoyed? ("How can I meditate with that!") Despair? ("This is useless. I might as well give up.") Plan? ("How can I arrange it so that doesn't happen next time?"). Minutes later, the door is still slamming within you.

Let's be honest. It is not easy to focus. We may be with the breath only five seconds before something snatches us away. Beginners often lose their meditation object for minutes before they realise it. This can be quite humiliating. You may feel you have a good mind. It may have given you a Ph.D., a highly paid career, and helped you raise four kids. But you find you still can't keep it in one place for more than 10 seconds.

It may be a shock to realise how little we control our inner world. But that is the truth for almost everyone. If we accept this, we can drop a lot of false expectations about ourselves. So when your mind wanders, bring it back without flogging yourself ("I must try harder"). Get on with the meditation, even if your mind wanders again ... and again ... and again. Keep hauling it back to the focus. It *will* get easier!

Meditation requires a sense of humour. Our minds always seem to wander more than we would like, and yet the meditation works anyway. Some thoughts have our number: they sling a noose round our neck and drag us through the mud. Laurence LeShan, the author of *How To Meditate*, says that if we had as little control of our bodies as we have of our minds, we would never get down a flight of stairs alive!

You can be pleased with yourself if you are reasonably focused for two minutes of a twenty-minute meditation. That is two whole minutes free from the tyranny of thought. Quite an achievement!

# ENTERING DEEPER STATES OF CONSCIOUSNESS

By meditating, we gradually deepen our ability to focus. First, we simply notice if we are still focusing on the breath or if we have lost it. Secondly, we go deeper into the non-verbal sensing of it: we pick up detail. Thirdly, we develop continuity of focus: we stay with it for longer and longer.

Focusing leads to states of absorption. This is when we are so acutely attuned to the object we are aware of nothing else. The day, the surroundings, our ego-concerns all vanish. We momentarily become one with the object. In this state, a profound sense of space and light can occur. Your body and mind feel extremely clear and stable. Each microsecond seems charged with life. It is quite unlike the vague escapism of daydreaming or "spacing out".

The Sanskrit word for deep focus ("samadhi") is a synonym for bliss. Every moment of focus, however brief, has a taste of joy about it. You are focused when your mind is caught by a snatch of song, when you enjoy a smile with a friend, when you smell a flower. Imagine that expanded a thousandfold. This is how the little pleasure of focusing expands into the big pleasure of samadhi.

Samadhi affects the body too. All our emotional negativities vanish for those moments at least. Our mindstate is so healthy that subtle physical tensions can release from head to foot. The body can literally·tingle with bliss. When the mind is unified, deep healing can occur.

Lovely as these deep absorption states are, they are by no means the end of the road. They are just experiences that come and go, like all others. But the benefits of focusing are practical and widespread. Focusing is the art of selective attention. We become able to place our attention wherever we wish, and to resist the inevitable temptation to sidetrack. Soon we find we have greater ability to pay attention to things in our daily life.

*"I find it easier to keep my mind on my study."*

*"I am more aware how I drive."*

*"I used to hate watering the garden. Now I consciously watch the water splashing over the plants, and it's a pleasure."*

*"I am more attentive when I talk to my children, and things are so much smoother between us."*

*"When something has to be done, I can just sit down and do it."*

# TRYING TO MEDITATE WITHOUT FOCUSING

When we relax, our minds wander. This can be quite enjoyable, but unfortunately it can wander anywhere. The mind is still indulging in thoughts when it wanders. Only by focusing can the mind abandon extraneous thought and become clear.

In any meditation session ask yourself, "Is my mind focused or is it wandering? Is it on the meditation object or not?" When your mind is wandering, you are just relaxed. Only when it is focused, are you actually meditating.

I meet many people who want to meditate without focusing. They may be able to relax by letting the mind wander, but they are unwilling to take the next step. Such people have caught the train to paradise and got out at the first stop.

I often have conversations that go like this:

Them: "I've been meditating for years, but I often fall asleep or don't get much from it. What can I do?"

Me: "Well, how do you meditate?"

Them: "I meditate on the breath for a little while and then I just let myself float away."

Me: "Why don't you try counting the breaths to keep yourself on track and stay alert? It sounds like you're too dozy."

Them: "I don't like doing that because it distracts me."

Me: "Distracts you from what?"

Them: "You know, that nice space ..."

Me: "But you say you fall asleep, or find yourself thinking about all kinds of things."

Them: "Yes, but concentrating is too hard when I'm in that mood. Is there anything else I can do?"

Other people focus, but compromise. They focus the way a mother "keeps an eye" on her children, while doing other things. I often hear the comment, "I can still count the breath while thinking about everything else!" People can meditate in this superficial way for years.

Some people say, "Sometimes I am right out of it (driving the car on autopilot, lying in the bath, long distance running). Is that meditation?" Definitely not! Meditation is not a particular spaced-out state. When you meditate you know exactly where your mind is, at that moment. It is hyper-aware, not blanked-out.

When I ask some people what they meditate on, they say, "Oh nothing. I just meditate." Other people "meditate" to relaxation music. But if their mind is drifting, as it usually is, they are not meditating. If there is no focus, or moment-to-moment awareness, they are just pleasantly relaxed, nothing more. "Drifting" is a positive state of mind, but limited in scope and vulnerable to disturbance.

By attempting to meditate, you soon discover how much or how little ability you have to focus your mind. If you can remain continuously with the breath for thirty seconds, you are doing very well. Without exaggeration, many people can't manage more than a second.

All of us can benefit from practice, and the challenge is very simple. Remember the instructions at the beginning of this chapter:

1. Relax
2. Choose one thing to focus on, and explore it
3. If the mind wanders, bring it back
4. Let all else go

## Basic meditation 1: THE BREATH

On the surface this appears a simple technique. You sit and count your breaths throughout the meditation. If this is all you do, however, the practice can be quite shallow. You may just be marking time. It is much more important to actually *feel* your breathing. Is your mind right there when the breath stops or starts? Are you noticing the changing moment-to-moment detail? Can you feel the reverberation of the breath in different parts of your body – your belly, diaphragm, chest or nostrils?

If you examine the breath with curiosity, your mind will be focused. You may notice fine sensations within you that can be fascinating. This meditation can eventually lead to an exploration of all the life-energies within us.

## *Instructions*

1. Choose a relatively quiet place and give yourself 15 minutes to meditate. Find a comfortable position that allows you to breathe easily. For most people a straight-backed, padded chair is ideal.

2. Spend a minute or two slowly scanning your body inwardly to release subtle tensions. Examine your eyes, mouth, shoulders, hands, belly.

3. Take a deep breath and sigh. Let your belly loosen. Give the breath room to move. Explore the movement of the breath within you. If there is a pause at the end of the outbreath, enjoy it. Let the breathing be spontaneous. Don't try to control it, or try to breathe correctly or make the breathing regular.

4. To stay on track, count the breaths up to 5 or 10, repeatedly. This helps to anchor the mind when you wander. You can either count on each outbreath ("one ... two ... three ..."), or double-count, on the inbreath and the outbreath ("one, one ... two, two ..."), or use the word "and" ("one ... and two ... and three ...").

5. When you lose the count or the breath, return to it without annoyance. If you are easily distracted, examine each breath more intently. If you feel sleepy, open your eyes a little or sharpen up your posture.

6. Let your body fall asleep. Don't be rigid. Have a background awareness of the sensations of relaxation – heaviness/lightness, tingling, gentle breathing, and so on.

7. Emerge slowly from the meditation. Sit quietly with your eyes open for a minute. Notice if you feel different from when you started.

# CHAPTER SEVEN

# POSTURE AND BREATHING

When I mention the word "posture" in class, at least one person shuffles guiltily and attempts to "sit up straight". Posture is important in meditation, but it is very misunderstood. Many people feel they can never meditate because they can't sit in the classical cross-legged lotus position, for example.

What matters is not the posture we take, but how we hold ourselves in it. In fact, we can meditate in any posture. We can meditate sitting in a chair or on the floor. Or walking, fast or slow. Or lying down, on our side or on our back. Or standing. Or in any posture in between. These are all traditional postures that have been used for millennia in the East.

There are, however, guidelines. Your posture should be

comfortable (but not too comfortable), balanced and open (so you can breathe easily) and alert. You can't expect to meditate well slumped in an easy chair or curled up in bed, for example. The most important general rule is: don't slump.

The simplest way to relax is to notice the moment-to-moment sensations of tension and relaxation in your body. This is to be aware of posture. Does your body feel tight, hard and locked-up? Or soft, loose and open? Good posture "grows from within", as you become more attuned to yourself.

It helps to start any meditation by scanning your posture. Are you comfortable and balanced? Are you breathing easily? The chances are that you are not. Not perfectly, anyway. It is very valuable to spend a minute or two loosening the body up. In itself, this is a mini-meditation on posture. It could be the most productive part of the whole session.

"Having eaten and rested, the wanderer goes to a wild place and sits comfortably at the foot of a tree ..." These instructions are 2500 years old. They come from the Buddha, and emphasise the need to be comfortable. There is enough discomfort in the mind without stressing the body as well.

It seems obvious to be comfortable if you want to relax. Yet many Westerners go through agony for years trying to sit cross-legged. Do they feel it must be better if it hurts? They may assume that any "spiritual" discipline necessarily involves mastering the demands of the flesh, and that to be comfortable is almost a sin. These ideas are often not conscious. But they are all the stronger for being deeply engraved in our Western conditioning.

Meditation embraces the wholeness of our being. It attempts to integrate body and soul. The East has a profound respect for the wisdom of the body, and this is reflected in the physical disciplines of yoga and the martial arts. I analysed a dream recently in which the person dreamt that peasants from her home country were inviting her into the wheatfields to listen to the sound of the earth. Finding good posture should be like this: listening to the signals from within.

So be comfortable. Even in the Buddha's day, people meditated in chairs occasionally. They were called "seven-limbed" chairs: four legs, one backrest and two armrests. For many Westerners, a straight-backed padded office chair is ideal.

The chair should be low enough for you to have both feet firmly on the ground. To relax to the point of sleep, you need to feel stable. If you are a small person, you may find your feet dangle. In this case, prop up your feet with cushions. Even better, cut down the legs of the chair to the right size. It is worth it, if you are going to do a lot of meditating!

Some people like armrests and some don't. Armrests can prevent the shoulders slumping, and give you a feeling of security. They are good for the "elderly and infirm", or for you, at any age, if you happen to feel elderly and infirm.

When sitting in a chair, the right-angle between torso and legs can block the breathing a little. This can be overcome somewhat by spreading the legs apart and letting the belly hang out: samurai position.

Sitting on the floor is excellent if you are supple and relatively fit. However, most people don't sit well on the floor, so let me first describe how *not* to do it.

When sitting on the floor, you may start with good posture, but soon your shoulders may slump and your chest collapses. This blocks your breathing and creates a physiological depression in the body. Try it out. Let your shoulders slump right now, and notice how your mood changes.

Slumping shoulders induce a blocked, low-energy state, which inhibits the vitality of the body. You may feel a slight emotional depression as well, a kind of "leave-me-alone" mood. It is like lying in bed half-asleep when you don't want to rise and face the day. People who meditate a lot, especially in religious groups, may fall into this trap. They can shut down their body and mind, but it is not very refreshing. The posture reinforces a slightly depressed, escapist state of mind.

Zen practitioners make an art of sitting. They are a good model to follow, if you want to sit on the floor. They use big round cushions, about eight inches deep and solidly padded. Sitting on these lifts the hips well above the knees.

The cushions are so large they may tilt slightly as you sit on the edge of them. Some people place a smaller cushion, or rolled-up blanket, underneath them at the back to increase the tilt. This throws the hips forward a little, which helps prevent slumping in the small of the back. It helps keep the back upright and the shoulders open. The effect is similar to that produced by an ergonomic kneeling chair.

If you sit against a wall, it helps to have a small cushion in the small of your back, again to prevent slumping.

Lying on the floor is a good posture if you have difficulty relaxing. Some people are so tense that trying to relax in a chair would be fruitless. They may try hard but that is often part of the problem. It's easier just to lie down.

Posture gives messages to the mind. To lie down, for most of us, is to say: "Go to sleep". If we can overcome that conditioning and stay alert, lying down is a good posture.

Sleep, however, is very alluring. I often meet long-time

meditators who complain they always fall asleep. "How can I stay awake?" they ask. Since they can obviously relax, I suggest they change their posture, to try sitting up, for example, or to keep their eyes open. But my suggestions often fall on deaf ears. The demon Sleep has them in thrall: "I couldn't possibly relax like that" they say, and happily go off to sleep again.

So far I have described posture rather mechanically. And certainly, when we start a meditation, we have to spend time arranging the chair and cushions and so on. It is important we do this well, but it is only the first stage. When we feel the flesh and bones are settled, we can go inwards and listen to ourselves. We are seeking a feeling of comfort, ease and flow.

Good posture grows from within over time. I have often observed how the posture of good meditators becomes more serene and balanced as the minutes pass. As they shed the mental garbage, subtle tensions release and spontaneous adjustments occur. By contrast, beginners often slump as the meditation progresses. It is a sign their minds are murky rather than clear. They may be relaxed but are not meditating.

Good posture opens the body and gives the breath room to move. When we feel the breathing clearly, we find it rarely flows with perfect ease. There may be subtle blockages everywhere. These tend to loosen as we notice them. We can finetune posture by watching the flow of breath and other sensations within us.

Can you watch the breath without controlling it? Relaxed breathing is often erratic — now shallow, now deep, occasionally stopping. Many people find it disconcerting. They wonder, "Am I breathing correctly?" and memories of yoga classes and schoolrooms return to haunt them. Many can't watch the breath objectively, they want to "make it better". Some people are even worse. They would like to control their heartbeats, too.

To control or not to control? Our minds are often at odds with our bodies. We are usually not aware how much or how little we try to dominate our bodies. The habit builds up over decades. Some people hold themselves very tight. Others are more trusting. Some people learn meditation because "I want to make myself relax". Others "let themselves" relax. The latter usually do better.

Notice how your breathing feels when you are almost asleep. Or look at that of a sleeping baby. It is unlikely to be regular. The whole body expands and contracts. There may be the odd deep sigh, and times when the breathing stops. The inner feeling is one of timeless space and movement without boundaries. This is relaxed breathing. Become familiar with this feeling.

As an infant grows, it learns to inhibit the flow of life within. Certain emotions are too overwhelming or socially unacceptable to be allowed to surface. The simplest way to suppress them is make the body rigid. This chokes off the breathing, which becomes habitually jerky, stiff and nervous. Much of the tension in our body and breathing is the continual struggle to suppress "unacceptable" emotion. This is spontaneous feeling that doesn't fit your (or others') view of yourself.

Meditation should be a gradual loosening of unnecessary control. This can be quite difficult. The entrenched bureaucrats of former communist states want to stay in control, and our nervous systems do too. If chronic anxiety and hard work have "got you where you are today", you are naturally reluctant to give it up. Your doctor may tell you to relax, but your conditioning says, "No. Hang on".

Many people try to relax by controlling the whole process. They try to find the "correct" way to breathe.

They may find various techniques which encourage them to control the breath: yogic deep breathing, for example, or counting the breaths in certain patterns. Or they try to make their breathing smooth and regular.

These are good concentration exercises to settle the mind. But they are still control mechanisms. It is good to take a step further and let the breathing be free. We still require discipline, but only to dismantle the rigidity that blocks the spontaneity of the breath.

"I thought I had to breathe deeply to relax" people often tell me. Two or three deep breaths, or a minute of yogic breathing, to start a meditation are good. But relaxing is like sleep. We don't control our breathing when asleep. Nor do we need to control it as we relax. Meditation is control of the mind, not the body.

Control is not automatically "bad", or freedom "good". Obviously we need a balance. However, Westerners usually err on the side of control. Christianity emphasises man's dominion over Nature. Although we may no longer be outwardly Christian, that attitude lingers. We still assume we should master ourselves and the world. Even the environmental movement often has the tone: "This is ours. We should care for it better."

The Eastern assumptions are quite different. They assume we are Nature, and one with Nature. The inner path is to better understand Nature (and therefore God), so we can operate in harmony with the forces around us. This means putting our ears to the ground and listening.

The breath and the body are wise. Unlike our personal egos, the body has been around for tens of thousands of years. It knows what to do if we give it half a chance. We just have to get the interfering mind out of the way.

In Zen, they say "If your back was perfectly straight, you would be enlightened." Perfect posture means perfect health and inner harmony. We may want to impose good posture or an enlightened mind on ourselves, but it can't happen that way. Perfect balance comes by listening with humility to the inner wisdom of our flesh and bones. Or, at the most basic level, being aware of posture and breathing.

# Basic meditation 2: BODYSCAN

In any meditation, it helps to have something systematic to do. Here we scan the body in deliberate stages from top to bottom, or bottom to top. Bodyscan is a meditation on posture and breathing. It is an excellent practice in its own right, and it can be used as a preliminary to other techniques.

Divide the body into seven regions and deliberately shift from one to the next. In the previous meditation, we explored the sensations of the breath to keep the mind engaged. In this one, we examine all and any sensations that arise in each part of the body. These could be pain, tingling, heat, tension, the pulse, moisture — anything at all.

You can scan the body up or down, quickly or slowly. You could shift from region to region with each outbreath. Or you could count five or ten breaths (or more) in each region.

## Instructions
1. Sit comfortably and shake your body loose. Casually survey your body and release any obvious tensions. Take a couple of deep breaths, and let go completely as you breathe out.

2. Scan the body at your own speed: one, five or 10 breaths to each region. Become interested in the subtle detail:

Scalp and forehead
The face and lower part of the head
Neck, throat, shoulders, arms and hands
Chest and back
Diaphragm and solar plexus
The belly
Hips, legs and feet

3. Centre on the flow of the breath anywhere in the body: belly, chest, throat or nostrils. Count the breaths, as in the previous meditation. Be aware of the background sensations of relaxation — heaviness, tingling, expansion etc.

4. Repeat Steps 2 and 3 as you wish. Alternatively, you may want to scan the body in an upwards direction. Scanning downwards is relaxing in effect. Scanning upwards raises energy and keeps you more alert.

# CHAPTER EIGHT

# ALPHA AND BETA BRAINWAVES

Our thoughts affect our bodies instantly. We soon notice this when we meditate: certain thoughts speed us up; other thoughts wind us down. If we want to relax, it helps to recognise the thoughts, or the states of mind, that allow this to happen.

With practice, we soon learn to recognise the physical signs of relaxation. The body feels heavy and loose, the skin may tingle, the breathing is light and so on. The next stage is to know what is happening mentally. It helps to know when the mind is in the alpha brainwave state, and when it is in beta.

The brain emits electrical impulses continuously. These are classified according to their frequency. When you are awake, the brainwaves follow faster rhythms (13-30 cycles per second) and are called beta; the slower rhythms (7-13 c.p.s.) are called alpha. Sleep rhythms are theta and delta. These different mindstates have quite different functions.

Beta is an active, thinking mindstate. It is busy. We are usually in beta most of the time we are awake. When in beta, we are able to think, talk, handle many different stimuli at once, and speculate about past and future events. It is associated with the left side of the brain.

Alpha is the opposite. It is relaxed. It is a receptive, sensing or feeling state. When sensing outweighs thinking — when biting into a peach, for example, or listening to falling rain — we are in alpha. When we feel an emotion "in our gut", rather than thinking about it, alpha predominates.

Alpha is most likely to occur when we are in the present, in the senses and in touch with ourselves and our surroundings. It is associated with the right side of the brain.

In alpha, we are just "being" rather than "doing". It occurs when we let ourselves open up and allow the world (and our own feelings) to enter. It is more passive, vulnerable and trusting — like the mindstate of a little child.

When "doing", our attention goes outwards. It is when we respond to, and try to change, things around us. This is more exhausting than the passivity of alpha. We need time in alpha to recover from beta.

In brief, alpha is when we are sensing or feeling; beta is when we are thinking. Alpha is in the present; beta is in the past or future. Alpha is in touch with here and now; beta is in touch with concepts. Alpha is mentally receptive; beta is mentally active.

Extravagant claims are made for alpha. It is sometimes called a "superconscious" state, and various mind training seminars claim we need it for psychic powers, self mastery, and getting what you want out of life. Yet it is completely ordinary. All of us spend maybe an hour or two in alpha every day.

Alpha always occurs just before and after sleep. In that moment when you flake out on the bed after a long day your thoughts drift away. You notice the little aches and pains of the body, the cool sheets. You are just there — in the senses, in the present.

When we are relaxed and aware, we are likely to be in alpha: walking in the park, listening to music, arranging flowers. It is when we unwind with a cup of tea and day-dream, or are absorbed in craftwork. We are likely to be in alpha whenever we "lose ourselves" in something beautiful or fascinating.

Alpha and beta can occur together, but they tend to eclipse one another. We can switch between them very rapidly. It may be useful to think of them being on a slid-ing scale. At any moment you may be in an 80-20 alpha/beta state, or vice versa, for example.

If you are talking with a friend, you are likely to be in beta. You may try to simultaneously listen to a piece of music in the background. But you won't be able to get into it. The brain is in talking, not sensing, mode. You can still hear the music, but through static, as it were. But if you said to your friend, "Let's listen to the music", the difficulty vanishes. The dialogue drops away, the brainwaves can slow down from beta to alpha, and you can tune into the music fully.

You bite an apple and the taste floods your being. You are right there, in the present, in the senses, in alpha. Yet a moment later, you may think "These are great apples. I'll buy some more today." Though you are still eating, your mind is not fully there. You are talking to yourself and your mind is in the future: beta.

Talking and thinking may be exciting and stimulating, but they are rarely relaxing. The fastest way to relax is to throw the switch in the mind from "active" to "passive". In other words, to shift from thinking to sensing.

We may spend an hour or two a day in alpha. Because it is a relaxed state, we tend to drift in and out of it, with little control. By meditating, we learn to recognise this mood and consciously deepen it. If we were wired up to an electro-encephalograph, we could see the alpha waves becoming larger and more harmonious. There are many ways you can recognise when you are in alpha or not. People commonly report the following.

## ENHANCED SENSING

*"When I open my eyes, all the colours seem bright, as if they have been washed by rain."*

*"Those flowers are so beautiful. It was like seeing them for the first time ever."*

*"I never realised how tired and sore I was till I started to relax."*

## ENHANCED FEELING

*"In the meditation, I realised how much I loved and appreciated my children."*

*"I realised I was still upset by an incident at work this morning. I thought it had washed over me."*

*"I felt quite emotional in that meditation. Is that right?"*

## TIME SLOWING DOWN

*"I heard every note of that music, and the spaces in between. It resonated through my whole body."*

*"My breathing seemed to stop for an awfully long time.*

*It was probably only a few seconds but it felt like ages. It was lovely. I didn't want to breathe again."*

*"Was that meditation 30 minutes? It felt like five!"*

# PASSIVE, RECEPTIVE STATE OF MIND

*"I heard that person coughing, but it didn't annoy me. A few uncomfortable thoughts came up, but I didn't buy into them. They just drifted by."*

*"When I stopped trying to get results, it felt great. But I tried to stay alert, and I noticed all kinds of strange things I'd never noticed before. Like the sound of my breathing..."*

These effects may first be obvious in a meditation, but they gradually become more part of your daily life. Meditators in general report:

- greater enjoyment of the sense world
- a deeper and more varied emotional life
- a feeling of having enough time

The secret is simply to spend more time each day in alpha, whether we do it in formal meditation or not.

My days are often busy, and before the evening classes, I like time to myself. So I invariably walk in Kings Park, across the road from work. This is my meditation: watching the native birds skip through the flametrees, sipping the nectar; feeling moisture in the air after a shower; watching the sun's rays flash out from clouds.

I think these are the best moments of the day. They are full of deep sensation, and deep feeling. They feel timeless, though I know I will soon cross the road again and be back at work. It feels like I am reaping the rewards of a quarter century of meditation, just walking for a few minutes in a park at sunset.

## Basic meditation 3: MUSIC

If music is your meditation object, the usual instructions apply. Relax, focus on the music and when the mind wanders away, bring it back.

Many of us use music as muzak, or relax by drifting along with it. However, spacing out to music is not meditation. It is just a form of relaxation, without much clarity of mind. Meditating to music should be more like attending a concert. If we spend $60 for a ticket, we want to keep our mind on the music. If we do, we enjoy it so much more: we pick up richness of detail and colour we would usually miss. The music is more likely to evoke imagery or feeling which can deepen our absorption (if we don't let it sidetrack us).

People often ask "Is any music best for meditation?" Any non-vocal music you like will do. It can be fast, slow, tranquil or passionate. It should have a certain edge to it for the mind to grasp hold of. I often meditate to fast complex music. However, the quality of your focus is more important than the music itself.

New Age or relaxation music is often too insubstantial to meditate on. It can be designed to make the mind dreamy rather than focused. However even this can be useful to create an ambience while you meditate on something else.

## *Instructions*

1. Scan your posture and breathing for a minute or two. Get your mind into alpha before the music starts.

2. Switch on the music and enjoy it. Feel the detail and colour. If images or colours spontaneously arise, you can use them to deepen the meditation. Feel the music resonate within your body.

3. Ask yourself occasionally, "Am I still with the music?" Notice when you are drifting away. Notice the special "live" quality of those moments when you are completely with the music.

4. When the music stops, come back to yourself. Did you relax fully, or are you a little charged up? Are you holding your breath, or is it soft and loose? When you feel fully in touch with yourself, come out of the meditation.

# CHAPTER NINE

# MANTRA
# AND
# AFFIRMATIONS

**T**here is a childlike simplicity to mantra and affirmations. In their most basic form, as taught by the Transcendental Meditation organisation, for example, it is hard to go wrong with them. They can be learnt in 10 minutes and done anywhere.

These techniques "use a thorn to extract a thorn". They use words to stop words. Often our bodies relax, but our minds babble on: commenting, worrying, evaluating. This internal chatter is the nemesis of many a would-be meditator. Mantra and affirmations are a way of counteracting this babble.

The principle is simple. We say a single word or a short phrase repeatedly throughout the meditation. This is usually said silently and in time with the breath. This gentle flow of often meaningless sound jams the airwaves, as it were, and stops other thoughts taking hold.

This may seem childish, but simple devices work well in meditation. This is why mantra and affirmations are so popular. Their simplicity is a virtue. They can easily be enriched by adding visualisations, concepts and actions.

There are four basic ways of using words: mantra, affirmations, counting and naming. These can be the actual object of your meditation, or a way of supporting it. We have already used counting with the breath meditation, and naming is discussed in Chapter 13. In this chapter, we look at affirmations and mantra. As there is more to be said about mantra, I will deal with affirmations first.

# AFFIRMATIONS

Here are some simple affirmations:

SLOW DOWN
LET GO
PEACE AND LOVE
RELAX
WAKE UP
LET IT BE
WARM AND HEAVY

It is important not to "think about" the affirmation. You say it silently and continuously while your primary focus is on the breath or the body. An affirmation is like wallpaper, providing background atmosphere.

For example, you may focus on the sensations in your hands as you say "warm and heavy". With repetition, the words become a patter of almost meaningless sound. It is like singing a song and entering its mood, without reflecting on the meaning of the words.

Yet you can be quite alert, focusing on your hands. Your hands are very sensitive, and as you relax, the feelings change. Your hands may well start to feel heavy or warm. It matters little if they do or don't. You may instead feel tingling or puffiness or pressure or the texture of your skin against your clothing.

Focusing on sensations takes you out of thinking, and allows you to relax. The affirmation is just there to set a mood and frustrate the flow of thought. Many people do think about the meaning of their affirmation, but I don't regard this as meditating. It is thinking, which is a beta brainwave activity. They may feel good doing it, but they're unlikely to relax deeply.

We have a problem with language here. "Meditation" is not a very suitable word to describe the skills I teach in this book. In the English language, "meditating" generally means "to think deeply about a subject". A good Christian, for example, would meditate on a single line of Scripture to extract a deeper meaning. This is an accurate use of the word, but it is significantly different from my usage. I hope you can get the distinction. When I use the word, I do not mean "thinking about a subject".

Meditation in the Western sense, only becomes meditation in the Eastern sense, when the person moves beyond thought into the direct non-verbal feeling. In the Western monastic tradition this is called "contemplation" or, in the words of St Benedict, "divine listening".

Affirmations are often used by people who do not actually meditate. For example, a person may say repeatedly "I am a warm and loving person, who moves with confidence and grace." This is a useful form of self-talk that can counteract negative attitudes within you. But it is unlikely to produce deep tranquillity and clarity of mind.

# MANTRA

A mantra is like an affirmation, but with two important differences. A mantra may have no meaning at all, or if it does, the sound quality of the words is more important. Secondly, you focus on the mantra itself. Affirmations are usually said while focusing on the breath or body. With a mantra, however, we focus on its actual rhythm and sound quality.

Here are some common mantra:

OM
OM AH
OM AH HUNG SVAHA
SOHAM
OM MANI PEME HUNG
OM NAMAH SHIVAYA

Mantra are musical. They envelop you in sound and the rhythm carries you along. Colours and imagery may arise as you relax, and the mood is often comforting and sensuous. Mantra can be soporific, like humming a lullaby, unless you specifically aim for clarity of mind.

Mantra are more "mystical" than a less emotional practice like the breath meditation. They can easily raise feeling and imagination, and may have a magical incantatory quality. This appeals to some and discourages others. Of all the practices in this book, this is the most religious or exotic in tone.

To make mantra accessible, teachers have tried to demystify it. Benson in *The Relaxation Response* suggests using the word "One" as a mantra. LeShan suggests getting a two-syllable mantra by opening the phone book at random. You take the first syllable of the first name, then open the book again and repeat the process. You have a mantra!

The Transcendental Meditation group (henceforth called TM) insists mantra is a psycho-physical discipline and not a religion. It extensively funds research into the effects of meditation to support their point and has largely succeeded in changing the image of meditation in the West. Big corporations worldwide are now quite likely to invite business-suited TM teachers to help their executives relax.

Yet some mystery and consequent suspicion still clings to TM. I think they had a problem. Their product is excellent, but it is so simple that if they explained it, people may not take it seriously. Would people pay $3,000 for something so basic?

For whatever reason, they keep their mantra secret. Moreover, people are given their personalised mantra in an initiation ceremony, and are asked never to divulge them. This use of personalised mantra is the main feature that distinguishes TM from other mantra practices.

Naturally, rumours run rife about these secret mantra: that there is only one (or four or seventeen) mantra, that they give to everyone; that everyone in any particular year is given the same mantra; that everyone in their thirties gets one mantra, and everyone in their forties gets another mantra, and so on.

Christian parents often oppose the use of meditation in schools, because they suspect that a mantra is a prayer to a heathen god. I can exonerate TM on this score. I have heard many TM mantra over the years, and they are just what they say they are: meaningless sounds, usually of two syllables.

But do mantra need to be secretive at all? In the East, mantra are "in the public domain" as it were. They are on walls, clothing, in books, heard in the street and temples. They are in popular songs and on the fronts of trucks. They are engraved on rocks and flutter from flags. Kids know them before they can read.

There *are* also "secret" mantra that require initiation, but these are rarer. Different groups may have their own mantra, for example. Or a certain mantra goes with a certain practice. However, these are not tailor-made for an individual.

It seems that only TM uses personalised mantra. Even people who are sympathetic to meditation and mantra find this aspect of TM disconcerting. It hints at elitism, and suggests that the traditional mantra that have been used by millions of people for thousands of years are less than "transcendental" in effect.

Mantra and the breath meditation are the two most widely used meditations throughout the world. Most people have an immediate affinity for one or the other. The breath meditation is more cool, analytic and down to earth. Mantra, despite the de-mystifying efforts of many, is still more emotive and imaginative. This is just part of the nature of mantra. Although I teach mantra in simple form, it may help to know other ways of using mantra.

Religious groups tend to prefer mantra, which are more suited to raising emotion than the breath. Hinduism has a great tradition of popular sacred songs. They are like Christmas carols, and are often sung for hours by groups of devotees. These simple beautiful songs are often quite repetitive and mantra-like in effect. When Christians learn meditation they often feel an affinity with mantra. The "Hail Marys", the telling of the decades on rosary beads and the repetitive liturgies of church are similar in effect to mantra.

People may also dance to their mantra, as we know

from seeing the "Hare Krishnas" in the city streets. It takes a lot of energy to sing and dance a mantra, which makes it difficult to think of anything else. It is suitable for the young, or those with undisciplined minds.

In India, mantra may also be said very fast and loud. This is the high-pressure hose theory of mantra. It blasts everything else out of consciousness.

Mantra can be said out loud or silently. People often start out loud, and as they relax, the mantra goes silent and becomes an inner murmur. Eventually the mantra may stop of its own accord, and the person rests in stillness.

The very simplicity of mantra can be a problem. Many people find them utterly boring, and their 20 minutes a day becomes a masochistic chore. Mantra is the wrong medicine for such people, so they should try something more challenging.

Meditating on the sound of a mantra alone can be dull. Yet mantra tend to evoke colour and mood, simply because of their musical qualities. As you relax, the mind often generates imagery spontaneously. We can play with these to deepen the meditation. As I said, using mantra can be very childlike!

Many Eastern mantra are the names of God. Saying a mantra is like invoking an aspect of God and it may be interwoven with visualisation, concepts and religious emotion. Obviously this kind of mantra is not just a meaningless sound you say in order to relax.

Some simple mantra *do* consist of a single meaningless sound: TAM, OM, AH, HUNG. Others, just as simple, are the names of deities: RAM, BUDDHO, JESUS CHRISTOS, KALI. Others are invocations: HARE KRISHNA (to Krishna); OM TARE TUTTARE TURE SOHA (to the female Buddha, Tara); and OM NAMAH SHIVAYA (to Shiva).

Some mantra contain concepts in pith form: the great mantra of Tibet "OM MANI PEME HUNG", for example evokes the diamond light of the Buddha of compassion.

There are long mantra also, like the Lord's Prayer and the Catholic catechism, and their equivalents in the East. These are contemplative mantra. Although they have meaning, they stimulate a mood rather than speculative thought.

Mantra can be very flexible. Like the breath, they can be the basis for a more sophisticated meditation. It is easy to add a visualisation (of a deity), a concept (Love or Compassion), and physical activity (bowing, dancing or fingering rosary beads).

Done simply, mantra can relax you very quickly. It is like a child endlessly repeating a word to itself. They can even be done while active, just as you can hum a tune while doing housework. It can be disconcerting to talk to a Tibetan sometimes. You can tell by the way he turns over his rosary beads that he is saying mantra while listening to you!

# Basic meditation 4: AFFIRMATIONS

Beginners often find affirmations very satisfying. It is a simpler practice than the breath, and requires little thought or practice to get results.

We are quite suggestible when relaxed and tend to respond to our affirmations without realising it. For this reason, make sure your affirmation suits you. We try out two in the following exercise, but it is good to invent your own.

## *Instructions*

1. Get comfortable and scan your body for obvious tensions. When you are ready, take two deep breaths. Let go completely and feel the breath move within you.

2. As soon as you feel in touch with the breath, say the first affirmation: "SLOW DOWN". Say the first word on the inbreath and the second on the out-breath. Don't try to make your breathing regular. Fit the affirmation to the breathing. Pay attention to the words until they are ticking away automatically and effortlessly.

3. Now focus on your breathing. It may well slow down. This usually happens when you relax, but it matters little if it doesn't. Pay attention to the sense-detail of the breath or your heartbeat. This helps the brainwaves slow down into alpha.

4. Remain with "SLOW DOWN" for a while or switch your affirmation to "LET GO". The mood may change. You may find it easier to let go on the out-breath, or let go thoughts, or let go trying for an effect.

5. Continue with whichever affirmation suited you best, or invent one of your own. At the end of the meditation notice if and how your mood has changed.

# Basic meditation 5: MANTRA

You can go straight into a mantra without relaxing first. The mantra will sweep out the thoughts and the body will soon come round. You can say it in formal meditation or while doing the dishes, walking or buying the groceries.

You can use any mantra that I've noted in this chapter. The following three work well: OM AH is a good simple mantra (OM on the inbreath, AH on the outbreath). Another simple mantra is SHALOM (said on both the in-breath and the out-breath).

Longer mantra give you something to get your teeth into. They keep you more alert when you relax deeply. People particularly like the Tibetan mantra OM MANI PEME HUNG for this reason. It also has a good rolling rhythm that carries you along. Pronounced "Om Manee Paymay Hung", it can be said fast or slow, in time with the breath or your heartbeat or footsteps, or independent of any body rhythm.

## Instructions

1. Select a mantra and start repeating it silently. It usually helps to synchronise it in some way with your natural breathing or heartbeat.

2. Immerse yourself in the "texture" and rhythm of the mantra. Envelop yourself in the flow of sound. Weave the mantra into the sensations of breathing. Let the mantra carry you along.

3. Stay with the mantra. Notice when your mind is spacing out. If you are losing your focus, say the syllables more precisely or accentuate the rhythm. Enjoy yourself.

# CHAPTER TEN

# DEEPER STATES

The cartoon image of the ideal meditator can be exasperating. He sits effortlessly in a full lotus position and perfect health on a mountain, oblivious to the cares of the world. His thoughts, if any, are radiant and blissful. He seems light-years away from you, as you try to meditate in your untidy bedroom, tired and irritable after a frustrating day at work. "I'll never be able to meditate", you think as you succumb to one aggravating thought after another.

Unfortunately, there is some truth in the cartoon image. Deeper mind states *are* possible, and it is useful to know about them. Deep states usually last only a few seconds or minutes, yet they can have profound physiological effects. Nonetheless, the states closer to the surface are more valuable in the long run, since they lay the basis for everyday calm and awareness.

In the East, meditation is the path of "awakening". This means, in part, staying awake as your metabolism winds down and your body enters sleep. Since the brainwaves slow down as this happens, I find it useful to classify these states of mind as alpha, theta and delta. (This is a rule-of-thumb division, as the scientific evidence is not yet conclusive about theta and delta).

The first stage, however, is to be awake while we are awake (i.e. when the mind is in beta). Strange to say, this takes practice. We all know people who seem to sleep-walk through life. We ourselves, are often "not here" at times. We can drive across town on automatic pilot, and even work or relate to people in the same absent state of mind. Not surprisingly, this can create problems. Learning to be awake while you are awake is worth the effort.

The second stage is to be awake while you are relaxed (i.e. when the mind is in alpha). This is the stage most meditators are aiming at: to keep the mental clarity and focus as the body relaxes.

The third stage is to be awake in dream sleep (or theta). I prefer to call this the "body asleep, mind awake" state. This is when we are right at the edge of sleep. Our thoughts and our perception of the body may almost disappear, but we are still conscious. There may be dream images flashing by, and a sense of boundless space.

The fourth stage is to be awake in dreamless sleep (or delta). This is very difficult to describe, let alone experience. The metabolic rate can be extremely low, and there may seem to be no breathing at all. There is consciousness, but no images in consciousness.

This state is described as one of unshakeable bliss, outside time and space. It is quite rare, even in the East. Usually, it occurs only if the person has no worldly involvement, and is supported by a monastic environment.

The fifth stage is to integrate all of the above. This is to have the indescribable serenity of the fourth stage while arguing with your three-year-old over breakfast. St Francis of Assisi could do this. He felt the divine in the most ordinary things — stones, birds, the open sores of lepers.

For obvious reasons, I don't say much about the fourth and fifth stages in this book. We have to be realistic! However the third stage, "body asleep, mind awake" is certainly attainable for most people. It takes some training, but when you recognise it, you know "this is what that yogi on the mountain feels!"

The alpha state is common whether we meditate or not. Similarly, the "body asleep, mind awake" state can arise outside of meditation, but we notice it only rarely. For example, it may occur in a very light, clear state of sleep — perhaps as we are coming out of an afternoon nap. It is very beautiful and blissful.

Sometimes, as we drop off to sleep, we know we are still awake, but our thoughts are no longer rational. Dream images may zap by. We may feel disconnected from our bodies, or seem to merge into the bed. The body is asleep, but the mind is still awake.

People often experience this state in guided meditations. Students will say, "I seemed to be asleep, but I know I was awake. I could hear every word you said." Each time the instructor talks, it wakes them a fraction and keeps their head above water. Otherwise they would drop off.

They also say, "I must have fallen asleep about twenty times". In other words, they disappeared for a second or two, and came back, often because their head jolted forward. They were able to balance, if only just, on the brink of sleep. (Some people, on the other hand, fall asleep only once — but for minutes!)

Their bodies were asleep. A technician monitoring

metabolism and brain-activity would say "This person is asleep". Yet obviously, they were awake — still able to follow the instructions.

It is quite difficult to remain in this state without practice or without someone guiding you. It also takes time to establish firmness and clarity here. People generally slither between wandering thoughts, dream images and sleep at first.

When you can hold it, it is a delightful state: serene, clear, timeless. You have entered the palace of the gods. The concerns of the day may utterly vanish. The consciousness is vast and empty but also vibrant and alive.

The beauty of this state is that thoughts have almost completely disappeared. People often ask me in frustration and despair, "How can I block out my thoughts? I just want to shut them off." There are three good ways I know — all requiring practice, unfortunately.

The first is to become intently interested in something sensory (see Chapter 11). The second is to disengage from thoughts the instant they arise (see Chapter 13). The third is to be mentally awake, while the body is asleep.

Many people can't imagine being alert without thinking. Let me use an example to explain this. If you are lying in bed, feeling your partner's sleeping body against you, are you "thinking" about him or her? You may be quite sensitive to the warmth and pressure, and the mood it evokes, without any words or verbal analysis in your mind.

This is sensing without words: detailed awareness without verbal commentary. You can still be acutely aware of the elbow in your ribs, the strands of hair across your face. And you may also be aware of the mood: a calm joy, a subtle pleasure, or possibly revulsion or despair. This all takes place in the alpha state.

We can still remain alert as we drop towards the "body asleep, mind awake" state. We may notice we are losing our boundaries. We don't know how we are lying in the bed, or where our arms or legs are. We don't quite know where our body stops and our partner's body or the sheets begin. We may feel we are dissolving into emptiness as we drop towards sleep. The brainwaves are entering theta.

Yet we may still be conscious. We are not inert and dead. We still feel the subtle vibrations of being alive — a spacious tingling and warmth, like the hum of the cells — which seems to be everywhere and nowhere. The subject-object distinction vanishes. It has a mood also, even if we don't put it into words. It is something like "God! This is lovely!"

This state often disappears the moment we notice it, but it can become very strong and firm. With practice we can enter this state consciously, sitting up in a chair. This is the quality of that yogi on the mountaintop, and we can have it too. It is a different, deeper mode of perception.

In this state there is consciousness, but no consciousness of self. When we are awake, most of our thoughts revolve around ourselves: "My job, my relationships, my possession, my plans, my feelings". We do need to think about these things, but not every minute of waking life. "Do I need to patch up my make-up ... ? When she said, I should have said ... What am I going to do about ... ? I shouldn't really have another beer ... "

As we relax, we step outside this mental soap-opera. Achaan Chaa, the great Thai teacher, said:

"If you let go a little, you have a little peace.
"If you let go a lot, you have a lot of peace.
"If you let go completely, you have complete peace."

We let go most completely when the body is asleep and the mind is awake. If we actually fall asleep we don't escape our anxieties. They just churn away below the surface. This is why sleep can be so unsatisfying for about a third of the population. But if we remain awake on the threshold of sleep, any thoughts and anxieties evaporate instantly, instead of just going underground. Because the mind is not being agitated by thoughts, our metabolism may actually slow down more than if we fell asleep. This is why meditation, minute for minute, can restore the body more rapidly than sleep.

In this state, we are almost totally disconnected from the body, and the "I, me, mine" self-oriented thoughts. There is just pure awareness, love and acceptance. This state cuts off the chronic emotional negativities that support ill health in the body. They can't get a foothold in the mind.

Being relaxed is very good for health. It prevents the accumulation of stress during the day. But dramatic cures of life-threatening diseases are more likely if you can enter the "body asleep, mind awake" state. Meditation is good medicine, but some ailments need high dosages.

As the body relaxes, it releases bound-up energy. This is usually wasted in thought (beta), fantasy (alpha) or dreaming (theta). Our challenge as meditators is to use this energy for enhanced clarity of mind — to stay awake as the body sinks deeper into sleep.

My challenge as a teacher is to persuade people that this is worth doing. Our tendency is to drift into fantasy or fall asleep when we are this relaxed. We are so conditioned to this, that the idea of being disciplined in this state may seem unnatural and an imposition.

People will not enter the "body asleep, mind awake state" consciously unless they first develop an appetite for the preceding state: relaxed and aware. When people learn to restrain their wandering thoughts as they relax, and enjoy the increasing clarity of mind, then the deeper states automatically occur. As the Buddha said "If a hen sits on fertilised eggs, in time they are bound to hatch."

# Basic meditation 6:
# BODY ASLEEP, MIND AWAKE

This is the most effective exercise I know for taking people into the "body asleep, mind awake" state. People often use it deliberately to get to sleep. It demands both sharp focus and relaxation, and is often best done lying down.

In this technique we scan the body, but shift our point of focus every two or three seconds. This keeps us alert. We look for new sensations in each place, then move on before the mind has time to get bored. This practice is simple to learn, although it may seem complex at first. It may help to put it on tape. In this meditation, first move systematically down the right side of the body, then the left side, then slowly upwards and finally down through the centre. We finish by focusing on the breathing.

## *Instructions*

1. Choose your posture. If you lie on the floor, have your palms upwards, legs a little apart, and a small pillow under your head. Spend a minute loosening tensions within you.

2. Now move your mind like a spotlight round the body. Name each place, and try to feel or imagine the sensations there, however subtle. Move lightly, sensing and letting go, sensing and letting go.

3. Right side:
   "Right thumb ... forefinger ... middle finger ... ring finger ... little finger ... palm ... back of the hand ... wrist ... forearm ... elbow ... upper arm ... shoulder ... right upper back ... middle of the back ... small of the back ... buttock ... thigh ... knee ... lower leg ... ankle ... heel ... sole ... top of the foot ... big toe ... second toe ... third toe ... fourth toe ... fifth toe ... the whole right side of the body ... right side ... right side ..." (Notice if it feels different from the left. Rest there about a minute.)

4. Left side, as above:
   "Left thumb ... the whole left side of the body."

5. Moving upwards (more slowly):
   "Both feet and ankles ... lower legs and knees ... thighs and hips ... belly and small of the back ... solar plexus ... chest and upper back ... hands and forearms ... elbows and upper arms ... shoulders, neck and throat ... back and sides of the head ... crown of the head ... feel the whole body ... " (Rest there for a few seconds.)

6. Moving down and inside:
   "Forehead ... eyes ... ears ... nose and cheeks ... mouth ... jaw ... the whole face ... inside the nasal passages ... inside the mouth ... inside the throat ... the right lung (feeling it expanding and contracting) ... the left lung ... the heart ... liver ... stomach ... kidneys ... intestines ... sexual organs ... the whole inside of the body ... "

7. Feel the gentle flow of the breath. Let the mind settle somewhere within you and count the breaths for the rest of the meditation.

# CHAPTER ELEVEN

# BEING IN TOUCH WITH REALITY

P eople often express the fear that meditation is just an escape from reality. Certainly when we relax, the world seems different. However changes to the status quo can be disconcerting, even if they are positive. If you find yourself calm in a crisis, you may wonder "Am I becoming cold-hearted and unfeeling?"

If to "be in touch with reality" is to worry about things that haven't happened; fret over things that can't be changed; or react with panic to daily events; then the answer is "yes". Meditation is an escape from all of that.

Meditation is a relaxed and aware state. This may occur while stroking a cat or enjoying an apple. Are we out of touch with reality when stroking a cat?

How the world looks depends on our state of mind.

There is the world as we see it through the beta brain-waves. This is the reality of money, work, superannuation, getting the kids through school, and the Gross National Product. We can live entirely in this, if we want to. We could call it "male" reality.

The world looks quite different when we are in alpha. Here, the past and future have vanished. Alpha is when we are sensing, tasting, touching, at one with our bodies, and our feelings, pleasant or not. All this is as real and solid as a rock. Yet it is quite unlike the beta perspective. It is a more "female" reality.

And when we sleep, we still experience things. A dream is real to us when we are in it. Is this perspective without any validity at all, just because it doesn't fit alpha or beta reality? So which is real? The beta or the alpha (or the dream) perspective? And if both are real, do you think of one as being "more" real? Is it 80–20? Or 50–50 ?

Meditation enhances alpha reality. This can be disturbing for people who operate mostly from beta. People who live on high adrenalin levels often can't imagine being relaxed while awake. It is as if their bodies only have an on/off switch, and relaxing can only mean sleep and oblivion. "If I go into meditation, I may not want to come back. Who would then pick up the kids after school?" They may voice the fear that meditation is like an addictive drug. They may tell me of some one they know who "got into" meditation, went to India and was never seen again.

I often hear the opinion that it is dangerous to relax. I am told it can make you insane or a brainwashed zombie. I occasionally receive anonymous tracts through the mail warning me of this peril.

For some people, to be relaxed while awake is as foreign to them as Outer Mongolia. This has a positive side too. When they do learn to relax, they discover a wonderful treasure within them. One student said, "I never believed I could feel so good. I've been seeking this peace for 50 years, and I thought I'd never find it." All he did was follow the instructions and relax consciously for the first time in his life.

Alpha and beta views of reality are apparently contradictory, but we need both. They are like the male and female, or the yin and yang, of our daily lives. We need to oscillate between them, from conceptual thought to direct sensing/feeling and back again. One is not right and the other wrong (although it sometimes seems that way). What we are looking for is a harmonious dialogue of these opposing realities. Yet people are also suspicious of meditation for valid reasons. The catchphrase of this book is, "Be aware. Know what is happening." Unfortunately, many people do use meditation to blank out.

To be both relaxed and aware is a balancing act. If we relax too much, we fall asleep. If we are too alert, we don't relax. It is quite an art to be in that zone where they overlap. Many people, however, lose awareness as they relax.

Indeed, many meditators lose the plot altogether. They can sit in a torpor for hours: relaxed but dull. Or they may freeze in position. This is called "dead-stump" or "bronze buddha" practice. This numbed-out state is not refreshing. In fact, such people may feel worse when they "wake up", and may be reluctant to face the world.

Yet even this state has its attractions compared with the outer world. It is like a Valium doze. Meditators can perfect it over the years. They may say things like "I can switch off my mind whenever I want to". It always saddens me to hear this. It suggests repression of feeling, a denial of life and the stubbornness of an unhappy child. Yet it is a tone that is common amongst meditators in religious groups.

Do you lose awareness, either deliberately or despite yourself? It helps to notice the danger signs: your mind may become pleasantly cloudy; interesting fantasies may float by; you find you are no longer bothering to count the breaths; a seductive heaviness comes over you; you seem to be hovering in a beautiful crystalline space. It may seem like you've achieved what you wanted. Without self-discipline, however, you can't hold it.

You may realise you've been gone for a moment. You come back to yourself, thinking "Where was I?", then vanish again. These moments are lovely but so brief. If you go with them, you have a moment's pleasure. Then they disappear, or you drop into a half-sleep or aimless thought.

Meditation keeps you in touch with reality only if you remain alert. One of the best ways to stay awake is to meditate with your eyes open.

I train people by asking they spend the last minute or two of each meditation with their eyes open. It helps to keep the eyes soft, almost out of focus. They should be resting lightly on something in front of them — a spot on the carpet will do — to resist the temptation to scan the room.

Many people find this idea absurd at first. Initially they say things like "As soon as I opened my eyes, it was all over". If they are in a pleasantly fuzzy state, they dislike opening the eyes because they lose it. But that fuzziness is not meditation. It may take people a very long time to realise that meditating is to be both relaxed and alert. If we are alert with our eyes closed, it is no shock to open them.

Some people resent having to open their eyes, even for a minute, and want to know why. "It's so much easier with my eyes closed", they complain. There is a long list of reasons in favour of learning to meditate with the eyes open.

Meditating with your eyes open is essential if you want to become more relaxed and aware in daily life. You can meditate in company without being conspicuous: in wait-ing rooms, at bus stops and queues. You can meditate while walking. Having your eyes open gives more edge to your practice. You can more easily pick up moment-to-moment detail. It sharpens your awareness and you become more acutely attuned to the movements of the mind.

You can brighten up your meditation by briefly open-ing your eyes. You can check the time, if you need to, without disturbing the practice.

You can meditate on things of beauty. A rose, a candle flame or a crystal are classic meditation objects. You could also focus on a tree, clouds, the wind in the grass, the colours of sunset, rain falling, a bird in the scrub, sunlight sparkling off water, a dead leaf , a spider web, the night sky.

Meditating on visual objects has great advantages, even though it may not be as tranquillising as the mantra or the breath. It enhances our sense-pleasure and our empathy with Nature. It takes us out of ourselves, and counter-balances the introspective "navel-gazing" tendencies of some other meditations.

I usually do 15 or 20 spot meditations each day on things like those I've mentioned above. It makes life much more enjoyable. There is time, even in the busiest day, to steal a minute here and there.

One student told me: "Yesterday the office politics were horrible, and it was my task to sort it out. I felt sick and I had to escape into the park. I could only stay five minutes, but it was just so beautiful there. I was amazed that I could enjoy it so much despite the muck in the office. At last, I really understood what meditation was about."

Meditating with open eyes is a threshold many meditators never cross. When they get up from their cushion or chair, that's it! It means that meditation is something they can only do in private, like getting undressed.

Earlier in this chapter, I explained that we live in contradictory "real" worlds, which I labelled alpha, beta and
sleep. As we go deeper in our meditation, we can notice
different stages on the way.

In beta, for example, we may attempt to focus on the
breath or a flower, but we are not yet centred on it. The
object is just one of hundreds of perceptions flashing
through our busy minds. It as if we were running round
the office, trying to respond to everyone. This is the stage
of Intermittent Focus.

Gradually we become able to hold the object in mind,
but it is still a battle. We continually have to drag our minds
away from obsessive thoughts. This is when the office may
be in chaos, but at least you can stay at your desk and
attempt to work. This is the stage of Focus with Struggle.

Eventually we give up our involvement with other
things and feel at home with the breath or the flower.
This is when the office has quietened down. We still hear
sounds and people talking, but we can centre in our work
now. This is the stage of Focus without Struggle.

Most of any meditation takes place in this state —
centred, but still aware of events on the periphery. You
may still be aware of traffic noise, a stomach-ache, a nag-
ging problem, but you no longer react to them. You feel
detached. There is a sense of space between you and
them.

Only now do we start to feel or see our object in detail.
The subtle ripples and muscular shifts of the breath become
highlighted. Or when looking at the flower, we notice for
the first time the play of light and shade, gradations of
colour and possibly our emotional response to it.

If you are both relaxed and aware, you pick up fine
detail. This is the hallmark of good meditation. People
often say with delight, "I don't think I've ever looked so

deeply before at a rose (crystal, flame, driftwood, apple)."
It is amazing how lovely the world looks when the mind
is not cluttered by other thoughts.

A clear mind is not empty. It is a mind that sees clearly.
It is like having clean spectacles. You can see accurately, in
full detail, whatever is before you. This clarity of mind
endures after the meditation. People say:

*"When I come out of the meditation, the colours seem
so bright."*

*"When I come in here after work, I never notice the
trees in the park. But when I leave, they always look so
alive and beautiful."*

*"After I meditate, everything is heightened. It's almost
too intense, too real."*

It has many downstream benefits:

*"I always study much better after meditating."*

*"For the first time I saw what was happening between
me and my daughter."*

*"I can now see how I make the pain worse, and how to
relax into it."*

*"I am starting to realise how much watching the TV
news each night upsets me. I don't know why I do it."*

Meditation ultimately changes people's lives for the
better. It is not because they relax more and sleep better. It
is because meditation take the blinkers off. We wake up.
We see and understand what is happening. The mental
fog clears and the useless fantasies dissipate. We are in
touch, from moment to moment, with the physical sensations and emotions of being alive. For better or worse,
we are in touch with reality.

# Basic meditation 7:
# NATURAL OBJECT

When something catches our attention, the mind momentarily focuses on it and other thoughts disappear. This happens many times each day. This meditation extends this natural event into a formal practice.

I often teach this meditation by putting several objects on a table — a vase of flowers, a candle, a crystal, an apple or mango, a piece of driftwood, a multi-coloured silk scarf. It is important that the students can choose something they personally find attractive.

We can look at the object plainly, as it were, in terms of colour and form. However memories and associations often arise spontaneously the more we relax. We may find ourselves imagining the texture, taste and internal structure of an orange, for example. This can deepen our sense of empathy and oneness with the object.

We can boost this process using our imaginations. We can imagine becoming small and going inside the apple. Or becoming it. This can be a lot of fun. Here are two reports from students:

*"I was swishing around inside the segments of the orange, and the segments within the segments. It reminded me of the plump freshness of a baby's skin."*

*"I thought, how silly, I can't 'go inside' the rock. But I was there, and I really felt something of its structure. I almost know what it feels like to be a rock."*

## *Instructions*

1. Put something that interests you on a table at a convenient distance in front of you — not too close or far away, not too high or low. Close your eyes for two minutes and relax, using any technique.

2. Open your eyes. Keep the muscles loose and soft. The eyes may be almost out of focus. Let your eyes settle on to the object and explore it.

3. Name the object silently like a mantra each time you breathe out. Without effort and without staring, become familiar with it. Notice its colour, shadow patterns, texture, and so on.

4. Use your imagination if you wish. Imagine touching or holding it, going inside it or becoming it, or allow associations to arise.

5. If you wish, close your eyes and explore the object in your imagination. Continue saying the word to evoke the image. The detail of it may change slightly. If you lose the image completely, open your eyes again.

6. Occasionally scan through your body to make sure you are relaxing. If you are tensing up, keep your eyes closed for a while. If you become too dreamy, open your eyes.

7. Meditate on the object with your eyes open or closed as you wish. At the end of the meditation, notice how your body feels.

# CHAPTER TWELVE

# VISUALISATION

**W**e are fantasising beings. We live through our thoughts, hopes and fears. The world we see mirrors these inner dramas totally. We rarely, if ever, see the world plainly. We also share the collective illusions of our society, which are so pervasive we take them unquestioningly as real. As a technique visualising builds on this ongoing inner process.

I often feel presumptuous as I write this book. How can I hope to describe meditation adequately in only 40,000 words! I tell myself "Well, this is a book for beginners ... " And now I am trying to explain visualisation, which is an equally vast subject, in a single chapter!

So let's start with something plain and manageable. At bottom, visualising can be a practice, just like any other, to make the mind relaxed and alert.

Some people visualise easily. They may find the breath boring to watch, but they can readily imagine their child's face, a rose, a rainbow, a scene in the country. They can meditate on that instead. Focusing on something imaginary works just as well as, and often better than, focusing on something "real".

Right now, try it out. Read these words slowly and pause occasionally. Can you imagine an apple? What kind is it? Red Delicious, Granny Smith? Big or small? Feel its texture and weight in your hand. Is it smooth or waxy or slightly sticky? Imagine biting into it. Feel the resistance of the skin before it breaks. Is it crisp or a little soft? Catch the first burst of smell and taste. Hear the sound as you bite off a piece, and feel it in your mouth (and if you don't like apples, notice your distaste). Imagine swallowing it.

This exercise probably evoked something in you — a passing image, memory or sensation at least. Maybe you started salivating. You may not have had a clear picture. But you are almost certainly more tuned into apples than before.

Visualisation is an unsatisfactory word. The above exercise evoked all five senses, not just sight. A better term would be "sensualisation". Silva, the doyen of modern American mind-training teachers, suggests that you mentally set up a screen in front of you and project a visual image on to it. However, I find only about 20 per cent of people can do this easily. Not everyone is so visually oriented. Others can more readily evoke sound, touch, smell or taste. How did you go with that apple? What was the clearest sensation?

Even if the sense details are not clear, I find nearly everyone can evoke a feeling or mood. This is often stronger and more gutsy than sensory images, which tend to fade rapidly. You are visualising well when your body responds as if you are actually experiencing what you are visualising.

Read the following sequence slowly. Linger a few seconds on those images that grab you. Notice if your body responds — expanding, tightening, recoiling perhaps — and any accompanying emotion. Can you evoke the feeling or an image of:

- being in bed with your partner (or teddy bear)
- a melting ice cream cone
- intense pain
- the smell of petrol
- an open fire
- a flowering tree
- a baby's skin
- being at the beach
- a dead animal
- your grandmother

I am sure that some of these caught your attention more than others. You may also have found that some images arose spontaneously, without effort on your part.

A good visualisation works on at least three levels. These are imagery, emotion and body response. The first is obvious. It is an image involving one or more of the senses.

The second is an accompanying emotion that exactly fits this image and no other. You may love both your children, but your feeling towards each will be unique. An image that evokes this subtlety of emotion will hold your attention well — better than the sense images, in fact.

The third is body response. When you really enter into a visualisation, the body believes you're there. Try it out! For 10 seconds, imagine being under a cold shower. Now imagine being in a warm bath, or basking in the sun. Did you feel your body starting to contract in the first exercise, and expand in the second?

If you are visualising for healing, you need the emotion and the body response. Working with images alone is too superficial. I often find people who have a clear visual image — i.e. what we think of as a classical visualisation — may still be devoid of feeling or body response.

If we feel tired and miserable, we can visualise to give ourselves a holiday on the spot. We don't have to wait till Christmas. We can go to the beach or the country in our minds. I like to tailor these escapist fantasies to my exact mood. I ask myself "Where would I like to be right now?", and wait for the images to arise.

They are usually quite precise and different each time. Perhaps I want to be sitting under the hanging branches of a tree, at dusk in autumn, with mist around the hills. I want to be in the arctic tundra in midsummer. I want to be with my friend in New Zealand, having a cup of tea on the veranda.

In a good visualisation, every detail is like a holograph and contains the emotion of the whole. It is better to go deeply into single details, than attempt to paint the entire scene. Imagine the steam swirling from the cup of tea, or the smell and texture of the dead leaves, or the sound of birds in the distance. In other words, *be* there. Planning an itinerary for a trip through Europe won't give the same effect.

There are two distinct schools of visualisation. In one, you "make" the image arise. In the other, you "let" the image arise. These are sometimes called programmed visualisation and spontaneous visualisation. The exercise of projecting a picture on to an imaginary screen is a programmed method.

People automatically prefer one approach over the other. Someone told me he could even program his dreams, but the idea of allowing spontaneous images to arise was repugnant to him. Programming involves more conscious control: it is closer to thinking and the beta brainwave state.

Working with freely arising images allows us to create a discourse with our dream consciousness, which takes us deeper into alpha and even theta brainwaves.

Most people find it easier to work with the freely arising images. They can't evoke a perfect white rose on demand, but they can try and see what arises. If your mind is relaxed, the unconscious will soon deliver something. It may not be a rose ... possibly a daisy or a camellia will arise instead. And it may be slightly pink. Perhaps it is fully open, and past its prime. There may be some bruising on the outer petals. And there is a bug inside ...

The breath and mantra are straightforward practices. However, visualising can be very idiosyncratic, especially when you are working with freely arising imagery.

It may interest you to know how I learnt to visualise over the years. For years, I was a "cool" meditator. I rigorously developed close observation of the breath and the body and eschewed any imagery that arose. I was a pure sensation meditator, "in touch with reality" with no frills. But something was lacking so I took up the practices of Tibetan Buddhism. My training involved literally tens of thousands of prostrations, mantras and accompanying visualisations — not at all what I thought of as meditation.

Even worse, I apparently couldn't visualise at all. I sympathise completely with students who tell me, "Nothing came up. My mind was a blank." I was supposed to be evoking colours, male and female deities, crystal palaces, trees, animals, jewels, energy flows in the body, and I was getting nothing at all.

Yet I doggedly persisted, with little hope, and suddenly it happened. It was like a door flying open. The imagery had always been there, I just hadn't looked in the right direction. It was not at all what I expected, but it was very real nonetheless. The images didn't replace or compete with "reality". They were like a superimposition, or a double image overlaying it.

Once I knew how to look, my memory bank opened. I found memories arising with an extraordinary richness of detail and feeling from earlier and earlier in my childhood. For months, I consciously spent a few minutes each day recollecting the house I lived in until I was eight. I always found something new. The well was inexhaustible.

Over the years the imagery has changed enormously. Initially, I would get images of that day. With more tranquillity, the deep memories of youth, childhood and infancy arose. As I gradually worked through my past, I dropped through the personal memory bank into what Jung would have called the collective unconscious. The imagery now is indescribably diverse, strange and intricate. The entire universe seems to offer itself on a platter.

Our minds are always generating imagery. We don't notice it because the conscious mind is too bright and noisy. The stars are always there, but we don't see them when the sun is out. We usually only notice this imagery when we are on the borderline of sleep.

I had always been fascinated by dreams. Now I discovered some part of the mind was always dreaming, day and night, even as I ate breakfast, answered the telephone and worked on the computer.

A dream is like a message from the god inside us, telling us truthfully what is happening in the psyche. It generally tells us what is out of balance there. We don't have to go to sleep to tune into it. Here are a couple of "first aid" exercises. I particularly do them when I'm feeling under pressure.

Ask yourself "Where am I?" Sense your body and allow an image to arise that expresses the feeling in your body. This is what some students have reported:

*"I feel like a half-rotting jellyfish."*
*"There is a ball of lead in my stomach."*
*"I feel like a tangled bundle of barbed wire, shredded paper and old shoes."*

Usually it is a relief to recognise the image, even if it appears terrible. An unacknowledged feeling that gnaws at you from within is always more difficult to deal with.

You can ask yourself the same thing, say, in a pleasant meditation. It helps reinforce the state.

*"There is a soft shining golden mist all around me."*
*"A cool river is flowing through me from head to foot."*
*"I feel the cells of the body singing to each other. They have a definite pitch, and the feeling is soft like cotton wool."*

Here is a similar exercise. When something disturbing has entered your consciousness, ask "What is this?" and wait for an image. It may bring insight. I had a clear example of this recently. I put down the phone after an amicable conversation, but felt just awful. I asked myself "what is this?" and waited for the image to arise. It soon came. The image was that I had eaten mouldy fruitcake (the unconscious has a great sense of humour!).

Insight immediately followed. The woman I spoke to had great ability (the fruitcake), which I felt was flawed by emotional dishonesty (the mould). The image told me how I instinctively responded to her. Knowing this made it easier to relate to her in future.

People often visualise without knowing how to medi-
tate. After all, it is quite easy to fantasise. We all do it, but it
is often quite superficial. A good visualisation is more than
daydreaming and wishful thinking.

As a teacher, I am interested primarily in the student's
quality of mind. Is it relaxed, clear, capable of good focus,
able to resist sidetracks, flexible, serene? The meditation
object is just a device towards this end. Without developing such a quality of mind, nothing much is possible.

Visualisers are often so entranced by the imagery produced that they don't notice their quality of mind. It may
be excited, manipulative, clinging, scattered or anxious. I
often meet people who visualise (and use affirmations) in
a tight, controlled way that doesn't seem meditative to me.
If they are visualising to achieve some goal, they may be
anxious and tense about it. In any meditation, we should
first aim for an open gentle state of mind. The image
comes second.

I am often asked "Are there meditations for curing
cancer?" There are meditations for this purpose. However
90 per cent of the benefit of any meditation comes from
our ability to relax deeply with a clear mind. Fear, anger,
sorrow and desire all vanish when we relax. At such times
we are at peace with ourselves and others, enjoying the
bliss of just being. What could be more healthy than to
spend hours in this state?

Healing visualisations can enhance this effect. But if the
person cannot even relax, a visualisation will be little
more than a feel-good "head trip". This is not without
value, but it is unlikely to help cure cancer, for example.

I usually teach visualising towards the latter part of a
course. People visualise best when they have a basic
understanding of calm and awareness to build on. Here
are a couple of simple healing meditations.

1. **Balls of light.** Imagine a beautiful ball of (white, gold, blue) light above your head. Have you got it? A similar ball below your feet ... to the left ... to the right ... in front ... behind. Imagine these lights merging and enveloping you in soft protective light. The light penetrates your body like the rays of the sun. Feel it around you as you move through your day.

2. **Diamond light.** This is a similar exercise. Imagine a pearly white or crystal-clear light streaming from space into the crown of your head. Imagine it as light or as sparkling spring water flowing right through your body, flushing out the darkness and pain. Direct the light where it is needed. Finally let the light settle in your heart and radiate through every cell of your body, expanding into the personal space around you.

---

# Basic meditation 8: VISUALISATION

Visualisations can be very simple (a point of white light in space, for example) or elaborate. Regardless of your inclinations, it helps to train on simple things first. There are various sequences you can practise with:

- the colours of the rainbow
- the four elements (air, earth, water, fire)
- objects of the five senses
- lifeforms, from viruses up
- recalling the sense details of the day — colours, smells, tastes, tactile sensations, sounds and the emotions around each.

This kind of practice develops the skill to build elaborate visualisations at will. The simplest of these is visualising colour. Some people easily evoke pure colour. Others prefer to evoke objects of that colour. You could also do the meditation below with any of the above sequences.

It is not important to "see" colour clearly, the feeling generated is sufficient. All that matters is to have the mind absorbed, so it doesn't wander to other things. Colour is just a device to hold the mind. Even attempting to sense something that is beyond your perception still focuses the mind.

## Instructions

1. Make yourself comfortable and relax, eyes open or closed.

2. Start working slowly through the colours of the spectrum, beginning with red. Say the word "red" each time you breathe out. Wait for a particular shade of red, or the memory of a red object to arise. When it does, explore the mood of it, without tensing up. Enjoy it for a minute.

3. Work through the colours of the rainbow, spending a minute on each: red ... orange ... yellow ... green ... blue ... violet (or purple) ... white. Notice that some colours or objects come to mind more readily than others.

4. Now go deeper into the colour that most appealed. Imagine the quality of that colour radiating throughout your body. Play with any associations that arise. Continue saying the word like a mantra. Don't try to achieve anything. Make sure your body doesn't tense up.

5. Let the colour go and let your mind rest with the sensations of the body for a minute or two. Notice your state of body and mind before you emerge.

# CHAPTER THIRTEEN

# "JUST WATCHING"

Often we have meditations that seem to consist of nothing but distractions. Every sound, thought and ache in the body rips us away from the breath or the mantra. Yet in time we realise there are no distractions. It is all grist for the mill. The secret is to "just watch".

Early in a course, if someone coughs during a meditation, I often see faces and bodies tightening round the room. People are obviously irritated and feel they have to "start again". Later they may comment, "I was fine until ... someone moved ... that plane went over ... I thought about work ... my back started aching". They may speculate that meditating is really not possible in the city. If only they were on holiday in the country, in good health and away from the kids, then, of course, they could meditate.

Yet two or three weeks later, a subtle change occurs, which often goes unnoticed at first. The "distractions" are still there, but they no longer distract:

*"My neck still aches, but I feel more relaxed anyway."*

*"That car alarm startled me at first, but I soon got used to it."*

*"I was glad when someone over there coughed. It helped wake me up."*

*"I thought it would be useless coming to meditation today. I've got this horrible situation to sort out tomorrow. But I put it in the back of my mind, and I was able to relax regardless."*

This lighter, more detached, attitude often arises during the week as well:

*"I don't know why I didn't go crazy at work on Friday. I just seemed to ride it out."*

*"I was able to tell myself — don't let it get at you — and it didn't."*

*"I no longer get so mad at the idiots on the road."*

Such people are learning just to watch the aggravations with detachment. They realise they don't have to react mindlessly. They find they can look before they leap.

We tend to blame our unhappiness on things "out there" until we realise our response can make the situation much better or worse. If a child scratches his knee, he may have a few moments of tears, and then forget about it. Another child may create a drama that goes on for hours. Which one are you like? How often do we find ourselves brooding all day over some petty insult?

Meditation doesn't eliminate the difficulties of living. If a man's business is collapsing, his son is going from bad to worse, and his back trouble may require surgery, his problems don't vanish when he meditates. But he can react to his problems in ways that don't give him a heart attack as well.

Buddhist psychology says there are 89 different possible mindstates within us. But let us be simple and say that there are at least two, which are loosely similar to beta and alpha. We have a passive mind (alpha) that senses/watches, and an active mind (beta) that responds to the perception.

Both states of mind occur in any moment of perception. The mind has to be passive to take in a stimulus. First, we see it exactly as it is – the bare truth. A microsecond later we experience the emotional tone and usually respond automatically: "That's horrible, that's nice, and so on". The mind then becomes busy, weaving thought and emotion around the original stimulus.

An Indian metaphor describes these two minds. It says each of us is like two birds in a tree. One eats the fruit (the mind that acts and enjoys life) and the other bird watches the first (and understands what is happening).

The bird that watches is always serene. After all, it doesn't have to do anything. It is also wise. It sees clearly. The mind that acts often acts blindly. This watching mind is sometimes called the witness, or the observer. It is our best ally in meditation.

Surprisingly, both minds can be present at once. We can react and also "just watch" our reaction. I mentioned this once and a woman said, "I know exactly what you mean. I got furious once, which I rarely do, and really let rip at someone. At the same time, there was another me, behind my shoulder, saying 'Is that really you?'"

If we can just watch an unpleasant stimulus, it needn't grow into a distraction. We can't stop "negative" thoughts and sensations arising during a meditation any more than we can make the whole world pretty and nice. But we can refrain from throwing fuel on the fire.

If you are meditating and a door slams nearby, you could say "Dammit!" and amplify the frustration and anger of that moment. "Why can't people be more considerate! They always slam doors when I try to meditate." Or you could just watch, with no unnecessary reaction or commentary. Just watch your body jerk suddenly and settle down again.

The noise doesn't bounce off you, or wash over you. It actually goes through you and changes the quality of your body and mind. It is impossible to block or deny it, you just feel a little different after it happens.

Nonetheless, it is possible to weather it out, like a gust of wind at sea. When we "just watch" we are not numb and insensitive, we are fully alive to what is happening.

You can also just watch your emotional response to the distraction. You can't stop the flash of anger, but you can watch it pass. If you don't externalise it, you may feel it within you, perhaps as a hot red flash or a sudden prickling on the scalp. It may well be unpleasant, but you can still watch it and let it dissipate.

You may then feel pleased with yourself for remaining calm. Even this thought may produce a body response — perhaps a satisfied loosening within you. Here you have another thought to just watch without commentary. As soon as possible return to the breath, letting the whole episode go completely.

Tranquillity comes not by changing the world, but from allowing the moments of emotional pain to die a natural death. They are like a shower of sparks from a fire. Most peter out in a few seconds, unless they land in something explosive. Like sparks, the negative emotions – anger, despair, fear, attachment – burn when they fall on you. If we can accept the momentary discomfort, they soon burn out. If we flare up, they can smoulder for hours.

Good meditators don't escape times of emotional pain. However, they can give those feelings space to be there and move through. They don't have to tense against them. After all, pain of all kinds is a natural consequence of being alive. We might as well make the best of it.

The best meditations are often the most difficult ones. If our day has been particularly harsh, meditation can be very useful. In rapid succession we may feel pain, anger, indigestion, frustration, despair. We may be touchy and easily agitated by noise or memories or thoughts. The breath may be hard to find, let alone enter into. So we try to sit back and watch it all come and go. We don't try to explain or understand or cover it over or solve it. We just watch/feel without reacting, or at least "just watch" the reactions.

The feeling may well deepen at first if you relax and allow it to surface. You may feel hurt or betrayed, for example. Or your whole body may seem a raging mass of pain. When you see/feel it fully, it may seem hopeless. And yet it may start to loosen as soon as you acknowledge it. We can drop a lot of tension once we stop trying to block our true feelings.

To just watch a feeling is not to "think it through". It means you sense its physiological effect, which may be tight, flat breathing, a dull pain in the gut, eyes crinkling to stave off tears, and so on. Emotions are just like physical tension. They will soften and move through if you give them space to do so.

To evaluate a meditation, ask yourself, "Am I in a better state now than when I started?" You may feel tired and miserable, but you may have been in hell when you began. So you can consider how you are feeling to be an improvement. This was a "good" meditation. If you felt good when you started, and much the same when you finished, then your meditation was just a pleasant wallow.

To develop a clear mind capable of watching the events of our inner and outer worlds with detachment, we meditate first on simple sense objects: the breath, a flower, music. Before we know it, we are also developing awareness of something else: our automatic like/dislike responses, which I have discussed above. They are usually quite obvious.

The next stage is more subtle and requires some self-awareness. It is to "just watch" our underlying moods or washes of emotion. Sometimes we may "wake up on the wrong side of the bed" or feel racy and euphoric. We may feel irritated all day for no apparent reason. We tend to be so totally immersed in these moods we hardly know they are there. They are like tinted lenses through which we see the world. Yet if we can just notice them with the same detachment and acceptance we have towards the noise of a slamming door, they lose their hypnotic grip over us.

There are ultimately no such things as distractions. It's all just life, and all grist for the mill. Certainly you should put all your free attention into the breath or whatever. But if something else grabs you, just watch your reaction. Are you tightening or loosening ? How quickly can you let it go ?

Certain thoughts and sensations get us in a stranglehold each time they arise, yet even they pass in time, whether we battle with them or not. Other thoughts catch us because they are so attractive ("Wouldn't it be nice if ... "). It is so much better if we can stand back from any thought, and look before we commit ourselves. Ask yourself "Is it worth pursuing this?"

The art of meditation is to watch dispassionately anything that arises in consciousness. With training, we can stand back and watch the endless stream of thought, sensation and feeling flow through us, without getting involved. If we can let everything go, nothing will stick in our minds unless we want it to, and no single thing will be a threat or temptation. There can be serenity in the midst of chaos. Thich Nhat Hanh, the contemporary Zen master describes this state as being on the lotus in the sea of fire.

# Basic meditation 9: NAMING

In this meditation, nothing is a distraction. Whatever grabs your attention in the moment, becomes the meditation object. You focus on it for a second, name it, let it go and return to the breath. If you name a distracting thought, you can hold it at a distance, which disarms it. It doesn't matter how often you do this. Just recognise where your mind is: on the breath or on the distraction.

Naming is a meditation that leads to insight or self-awareness. It helps you see exactly what your moment-to-moment reality is like.

Naming can be done in many ways. It is usual to say the naming word two or three times, to slow the momentum of the mind. A naming word can be very precise or very general. Here are some examples of ways to name. Use any combination of the following that suit you:

If a thought from the previous day arises, you could say "past, past ... ". If it is one about tomorrow, say "future, future ... ".

You could name the relevant sense: "hearing, hearing ... (for sounds); touch, touch ... (for pains in the body); thinking, thinking ... ;" and so on.

You could label the emotional state: "sad, sad ... tired, tired ... bored, bored ... ". You could name your response: "Like, like ... dislike, dislike ... ".

You could name the exact object of the thought: "Mary, Mary ... assignment, assignment ... Bosnia, Bosnia ... coffee, coffee ... ".

## *Instructions*

Do any regular meditation. If the mind wanders, see where it goes. Shift your attention to the distraction, and name it, two or three times. Then return to the meditation object.

Don't pursue thoughts or get interested in them. Don't speculate "Why am I thinking about this?" Be quite loose and relaxed as you shift attention from the meditation object to the distraction and back again.

Don't hold a tight focus and censor out some things. Let anything come into consciousness, including those you habitually try to ignore. Literally everything is grist for the mill. "Headache, headache ... sadness, sadness ... tinnitus, tinnitus ... dogfood, dogfood ... ".

Learn to see all things equally and with detachment. This is your experience of life, right here and now. Can you accept it? Or do you want to pick and choose?

As you continue, the extraneous thoughts may become less insistent. You may want to remain with the breath, or enjoy the spaces where there are no thoughts.

# Basic meditation 10: CLEARING

This meditation is similar to the one above. In "Naming" we focus on the breath or the distraction. In "Clearing" we focus on nothing at all except the process of letting go. "Naming" is good when the mind is hounded by distractions; "Clearing" is an advanced practice to be done when the mind is especially strong and clear.

We usually focus on an object to help us abandon all other thoughts. When the mind is strong, however, we can even abandon the object and simply let the mind be open. All we have to do is be vigilant and discard whatever arises in the mind. So we focus on letting go, letting go and letting go. We continually try to disconnect and empty the mind.

Images may help to illustrate this process: this meditation is like sweeping clear a courtyard in a wind. As we brush aside the dead leaves of our thoughts, others blow in from behind.

Alternatively we can regard the mind as a stream of consciousness, with our thoughts like the leaves and debris floating by it. As soon as you notice you have picked a thought out of the stream, throw it back in again.

Or we can regard the mind as like a mirror. It is perfectly clear in itself, yet it reflects all the details of the clouds that pass before it. We try to identify with the mirror (the watching mind) and not the clouds (our thoughts).

Because in this meditation we are continually emptying our minds, unusual sensations, insights and memories that would normally never reach consciousness, may surface. It can be quite a challenge to drop them. As soon as you pick something out of the stream, you have lost the meditation.

"Clearing" is quite unique. Unlike most other practices, we don't focus on an object or image. Even in the "Naming" meditation, we still focus on the distractions momentarily. This practice, however, takes us into the underlying clarity of mind itself.

## Instructions

Start by doing any meditation practice. When the mind is so clear that nothing distracts you, drop the object and let the mind be open and mirrorlike.

Enjoy the space, and let anything pass through it — emotion, thought, sensation, memory. Show no interest in any of it. Be aware of the slightest attraction or aversion. It may help to say the affirmation "let go" as you breathe to centre you.

See every thought, emotion and sensation equally, without preferences: a twitch in your ear, a childhood memory, a flash of sorrow, traffic noise, a thought about tomorrow, a great insight.

If a lot of similar phenomena arise — a train of memory, for example, or all physical sensations — you are selecting unconsciously. You are truly disconnected if what arises is diverse and passes in an instant.

If you suspect you are lost, then you are. Stop immediately and re-establish focus on one object. Don't drift.

Tune into the spaces between thoughts. Sense the consciousness behind the contents of your mind. When you finish this practice, your mind often feels bland, spacious and quiescent.

PART THREE

# MEDITATION IN DAILY LIFE

# CHAPTER FOURTEEN

# SUPPORTING YOUR PRACTICE

I hate to admit this: some people benefit from meditation without any practice at all. A woman whose car broke down coming to her first class said, "I was surprised how calm and philosophic I felt." Other people say, "I haven't practised, but thinking about meditation slows me down when I'm hurried."

Some people just need a taste of meditation. It is like lighting a fuse and off they go. But most people require steady practice over months to integrate meditation into their lives. To make good progress, here are things to consider:

1. Make time
2 Practise regularly
3. Tackle the inner and outer obstacles

4. Evaluate your results
5. Attend groups and talk to meditators
6. Go on retreats.

# MAKE TIME

"When is the best time to meditate?" I am often asked. The answer is "Anytime". Is there any time in the day you don't need to be relaxed and aware?

Meditate whenever you can ... good times are early morning and late at night. If possible, rise a few minutes earlier, wake the body up with a shower or cup of tea or exercise, and meditate. This is prime time, when you are most likely to have a lovely session.

Sessions late at night can be scatty, but useful. Don't meditate for too long, or you may find it difficult to sleep afterwards. All the undigested business of the day tends to arise in the evening. The stream gradually clears, so you don't carry that baggage to bed with you. You will sleep better and are more likely to awake feeling fresh and ready for a morning sitting.

Meditate throughout the day. There are many moments in which you can do informal and spot meditations: teabreaks, walking to work, sitting in a bus or waiting room, after the kids have gone to school or when you arrive home after work.

There is always time. The day is full of gaps if we don't compulsively fill them. I remember a woman who gave up her full-time job while attending a course. She complained she still couldn't find 10 minutes a day to meditate; she eventually found it.

If you make meditating a habit, like brushing your teeth, it will no longer feel like something extra you "have to do". It only takes a few minutes. The benefits are that you function better; you require less sleep and sleep better. These minutes of meditation soon "pay" for themselves.

## PRACTISE REGULARLY

Set a timetable. Be realistic. Make it attainable and keep to it. Rewrite it if necessary. But have something to aim for. You are unlikely to do well if your schedule reads "I will meditate if there is time and I feel like it".

A good basic timetable would be: one formal session of 15 minutes, five times a week; and two informal sessions a day. Any less and, while you will still benefit, your progress will forever be stop-start. You will still learn but it may take years.

## TACKLE THE INNER AND OUTER OBSTACLES

The devil within you is likely to throw every possible temptation in your path: no time, too busy, too noisy, not in the mood, and "what will my husband think?"

Women often say "I feel I'm abandoning my family". They may feel they should always be available to everyone. To do something alone seems to violate their marriage vows. So they try to steal moments of meditation when no one will notice. It is better to train your family. One student said, "When that notice is on the door, woe betide anyone who enters!" Even her three-year-old, who can't read, knows what the sign means.

You may have to overcome a lot of resistance: the ridicule of family or workmates, the fear of the new, your own doubts and uncertainties. Just to arrive at a class or retreat, or to sit and try to meditate at home, can be a big achievement for many.

# EVALUATE YOUR RESULTS

I often hear comments such as "that didn't work" or "it wasn't as good as yesterday". Unrealistic expectations and self-criticism are your worst enemies when trying to meditate. Here are some clear guidelines for evaluating your practice:

- Just look for improvement, not perfection. You may feel sore and tired at the end, but you may have been worse at the start. Ask yourself:
  "Am I in a better state now than when I started?"
  "Am I more in the present and in touch with myself?"
  "Is the body more rested, the mind more calm and clear?"

- Don't expect too much. Plodding, workmanlike sessions often bear fine fruit two or three days later. Conversely, you can coast for a few days without practising. You may feel fine, but are using up any credit you have built up. A crash usually follows.

- Don't expect every session to be perfect. Meditating is like learning to ride a bike. You have to fall off scores of times before you can confidently sail down the road. You have to chalk up those "failures" to get to the "successes".

# ATTEND GROUPS AND TALK TO MEDITATORS

A regular group gives you quality time and space: no distractions, no kids, no phone, a supportive place and supportive people. A weekly group meditation can give you the lift you need to practise at home.

Being around other meditators is inspiring. You can see what meditation is about in the flesh. Without the "people contact", your practice can be insipid.

Everything I know about meditation, I learnt from people — my teachers, students and friends on the path. I sit in on any group I can find wherever I am, whether Buddhist, Hindu or Christian. Even now, my students teach me as much as I teach them. The right people provide the best learning space you can find.

If we share experiences, we learn. However, there is a commonly held belief that we should never discuss our meditation with anyone except the teacher. I find this attitude a terrible hindrance to growth. It fosters isolation, misunderstanding and self-doubt, and incidentally gives great power to the teacher. For these reasons I actively encourage discussion in my classes.

If you can, discuss your practice with a teacher or other meditators. You could have quite unrealistic expectations of yourself or the practice. There is a lot to learn about meditation and your own mind. Don't try to figure it all out yourself.

Teachers and experienced meditators have been there. They know what is likely to happen. Sometimes it is not all obvious. What appears good may be useless and vice versa. Ajaan Chah, the great Thai teacher, said some students are like people in a chicken yard who ignore the eggs and pick up the droppings.

# GO ON RETREATS

The best combination of people and place is a retreat. You can relax the moment you walk in the gate. The disturbances of home and work are miles away.

A retreat is a place to be, not to do. Just to be able to watch yourself, without interruptions, for a weekend can have profound effects. It is a chance not to achieve something but for the body and mind to bring themselves into harmony.

Retreats are good for everyone. They can be like primary school or finishing school. Beginners learn the ropes while experienced people go deep. At some stage you will realise what meditation is about. When back in the world, you will know what to aim for.

There are retreats and retreats. Some are completely silent. Some are run like military camps. Others are laissez-faire: you do what you want. Some retreats isolate you from others. Some use the group spirit to accelerate the process. Some forbid exercise, others encourage it; and so on. I now know what kind of retreat suits me best. I prefer retreats that have a rhythm close to everyday life. This makes the return to the city easier. I like a balance between solitary and group work, silence and dialogue, free time and structured time. I personally like two or three hours of vigorous exercise each day — yoga, walking — to keep the juices moving. The weekend and week-long retreats that I lead follow this pattern.

# Spot meditation:
# ANIMAL LIBERATION

Here is an anti-meditation. It seems to undermine most of what I have written in this book, and requires, apparently, no discipline at all. It is actually a lazy man's version of the "Clearing" meditation.

We focus on nothing at all *except* letting go. If your day has been hell, and any attempt to discipline your mind seems like pure masochism, try this exercise.

## *Instructions*

Let go. Give up all effort except the effort to let go.

Don't try to sit correctly or follow any instructions.

Open the cages of the mind and let the savage beasts run riot: problems, pains, fantasy, fears, anger.

Let them go. Resist the compulsion to run after them, picking up their droppings.

Just give up. Do nothing at all.

Enjoy the relief of complete despair.

Don't try to achieve anything.

Tell yourself that you are incapable of productive thought at this moment. It's probably true, so do nothing.

Be like an irresponsible mother who couldn't care less about her kids. (They'll probably sort themselves out anyway.)

# CHAPTER FIFTEEN

# KITCHEN-SINK MEDITATION

**A** Zen master was once asked, "How often do you meditate?" He replied "When am I not meditating?"

Obviously the master saw meditation differently from the questioner. Even a master has to eat, go to the toilet, get angry and sad occasionally, has to deal with difficult people and noisy surroundings, get sick and die. Can he "meditate" through all of that?

Yes. If he is a master, he is alive and open to everything. He feels the pleasure and pain of life completely as it happens. No illusions. No escapism. Embracing everything. Clinging to nothing. He is fully present.

If one word describes meditation, it is "awareness". It is to be awake while awake, to be alive to the moment. St Theresa was once criticised for eating perch with obvious gusto. She said, "When I pray, I pray. When I eat fish, I eat fish."

Meditation starts with tranquillity but doesn't stop there. The formal sittings in a quiet room are just preparations for more stormy weather. Meditation often seems to be an escape from life. After all, meditation is tranquil. Life isn't. But we can't run from life forever. Life has a habit of muscling in. The trick is to weave the two together. We can do this by practising moment-to-moment awareness at any time of the day.

First we find we can remain relaxed and alert with eyes open. Then while walking, say, in the park or at the beach. Then while doing simple activities such as preparing a meal or having a shower. We soon find we can stay calm when someone presses our buttons. Boring tasks become less irksome. We appreciate moments of beauty as they arise, and have moments of clarity even in strong emotion.

Beginners have little flexibility at first. They say, "I couldn't meditate because:

- a dog was barking
- I could hear the TV next door
- I had a stomach-ache
- I've got too much to think about
- I'm worried about my mother
- it was a long day. I was too tired
- I'm angry with my ex-husband

Eventually they realise it is all grist for the mill. This is exactly why they meditate: to remain calm and aware in the midst of life.

The Zen master is awake. We, on the other hand, often operate on automatic pilot. This gives the mind a break, but blurs our perception of reality and so it is a mixed blessing. We can shuffle through the day not sensing or feeling anything clearly. What is even worse is that we don't realise it. We may not even know what we are thinking. Some days we're just not here at all. No wonder we have problems and are so confused by them.

Awareness doesn't come automatically. We have to practise it, just like any formal meditation. Our practice should start with simple things: noticing the sights, sounds, smells, tastes and textures of the moment, and our automatic like/dislike responses.

This is what I call kitchen-sink meditation. I particularly enjoy meditating while I prepare food. Sometimes I focus on one sense, such as sound. I listen to every sound I make: cutting the apple, putting the knife down, the squeal of the tap and the water running, the bowl scraping on the bench, a foot shuffle, the fridge door opening, the clang as I place something on the rack, and so on. I hold my mind to the task by saying the word "sound" silently each time I breathe out.

Alternatively I notice input from any sense. The texture of the knife, fruit, door handle, water. Or the glistening skin of a capsicum, patterns of light and shadow, a stain on the bench. Or the sensations in my arm as I lift something. I non-verbally ask myself, "Where is my mind right now?" It is amazing how rapidly your mind can disappear into thought. And how interesting the sense world can be if we focus on it.

You may ask "But is this meditation?" The answer is most definitely yes. In this meditation you are following the principle of the Japanese tea ceremony. Your mind becomes tranquil and awake by focusing intently on minute details of sight, sound, taste, touch and smell as they arise.

The same guidelines apply as for a formal meditation: be

relaxed, focus and bring the mind back when it wanders. In these meditations, the object of focus is broader than usual: the entire soundscape, or senseworld, for example, but it still has boundaries. When the mind escapes into thought, it has jumped the fence and needs to be recalled.

The Buddha said, "When eating, just eat. When walking, just walk." This is a very demanding exercise. It can also be enormously satisfying. Try it. Try to eat a simple meal, like St Theresa, fully aware of the moment-to-moment sensations. Awareness practices often create a brilliance and lightness in the mind that is lacking in tranquillity practices. This kind of meditation has no boundaries. It doesn't require a quiet room and half an hour carved out of the day. Anywhere and anytime will do. You could make any of the following a meditation.

1. **Hanging out the washing** (feel the wet cloth, the varying weights, the pegs, the wind on your face, sensations of bending and stretching).

2. **Changing the baby's nappies** (smell, texture, playful emotions, annoyance, etc.).

3. **Eating a meal** (sound, smell, taste, body movements, swallowing, etc.).

4. **Arriving home after work** (letting tension go, changing clothes, slowing down, feeling irritable or tired or relieved or excited).

5. **Having a shower** (sound, texture, sensations of pleasure, smell of soap, wet skin, then dry, and so on).

Hot on the heels of sensation come emotions. Our days are full of indescribable beauty if we choose to look.

Instead we switch on the television and read the paper. One black emotion can literally smother your world for years. Often it takes a critical illness like cancer to make people wake up. Such people often say they suddenly see what is important – feeling the dawn air, enjoying a short walk in the garden, a moment with a friend.

To become more aware is like switching on the light. Yet it has a price: it illuminates not just the lovely things in life, but the mess and confusion as well. So the Zen master gets angry and watches the anger pass. He feels sadness without being sucked down by it. He feels pain without self-pity or fear. Anyone who has been close to a great teacher knows how human they are. They are not plaster saints or bronze buddhas at all! But they are certainly alive.

People often say, "I seem to be an automaton, responding blindly to everyone's demands. I don't know who I am any longer." They may express this another way: "I wish I could leave all this behind for a few days and get in touch with myself again."

If you need to find yourself again, it helps to start with the basics. I remember once helping a stroke victim re-acquaint herself with the world. I remember her childlike fascination as she handled a piece of fruit and learnt its name again.

To ground us, it helps to come right back to the sensations of the present – to taste the soup, smell the wind, see the clouds, feel the aches and pains. It may not all be pleasant, but this is what it is to be alive.

# Spot meditation: BEING PRESENT

This is an exercise to help you find yourself if you feel scattered or "not with it". It shifts the mind quickly from thought into the immediate senseworld around you. It can be done anywhere, at any time. It is easy to do when you are active. I often do it while:

- brushing my teeth
- cleaning up the room
- preparing to go out
- shopping in the supermarket

## *Instructions*

Ask yourself "Where am I?" Shift the mind from thought into sensations.

Notice how your attention moves from point to point — holding the toothbrush, turning the tap, hearing the sound of running water, feeling the movement of the arm as you lift, the tang of the toothpaste in your mouth.

Also notice the emotional tone: liking/disliking, hurried, restless, enjoying, tired, excited. Watch these with equal detachment, as they pass before you.

Notice how quickly the mind can escape back into thought. Draw it back to any immediate sensation, however trivial.

Passively observe the sensations and emotions that come and go as long as you wish. Don't think or analyse. As you notice what you are doing, you may find your movements becoming more harmonious.

## ■ CHAPTER SIXTEEN ■

# WALKING MEDITATION

**W**alking is a natural meditation that people do without realising it. A dawn stroll by the river or a ramble round the backstreets after work may be your way of relaxing. It gives you time to get in touch with yourself or nature.

You may not realise it but you are following in the footsteps of the Indian holy men of old. The students of the Buddha were not monks — that came later. They were "wanderers" or "homeless ones", who brushed the dust of city life from their feet and roamed.

Walking is as ancient a meditation posture as sitting. Australian Aborigines go on walkabout. American Indians go on a spirit quest. Young men and women leave the cozy certainties of home to find themselves. Walking reminds us of our nomadic roots, when we owned nothing and faced each day afresh.

"Leave your homeland to awaken" said the Buddha. His students were encouraged to spend no more than three days in one place (except during the rainy season). So they walked a lot and developed it into conscious meditation practices. It is just as easy to be relaxed and aware while walking as it is while sitting.

Some of these practices are quite sophisticated. Zen monks may walk in a circle, synchronising their steps. A Burmese monk may walk extremely slowly, verbally noting each micro-movement of the foot. Kung Fu and Tai Chi are developments of the Buddhist standing and walking meditations. (The first Zen patriarch of China is the founder of Kung Fu.)

Later I will give instructions for informal walking meditation — walking to the shops, for example. But let me describe the formal practice first, to illustrate the principles.

Since walking is a meditation posture, just like sitting or lying down, the usual guidelines apply — comfort, balance and alertness. We aim to walk comfortably with no excess tension. The body should be straight and balanced, to allow free movement.

It is usual to walk back and forwards in a room, or on a strip of ground about 20 paces long. This diminishes the visual distractions that would occur in a park, for example.

With Burmese insight meditation, you would walk slowly to notice the precise shifts in sensation as each foot lifts, moves and is placed on the floor. As you become more intent on catching subtle detail, your steps naturally become slower. It may take half an hour to cross the room. You would verbally note each stage: "lifting ... moving ... dropping ... placing ... etc." and eventually the start and finish of each stage.

This is a practice to develop exact moment-to-moment awareness. Extraneous thoughts can utterly vanish. Sitting meditation, on the other hand, tends to develop tranquillity, which is often soft around the edges. To alternate walking and sitting on a retreat combines yin and yang, and can give extraordinary depth and clarity.

Walking meditation may be easier to integrate into your life if it is done informally — while walking to work, for example. Since you are walking faster, it is easier to focus on the balance of the entire body, than on the individual foot movements. Notice how the muscular alignment of the body alters with each step. I usually anchor my mind on the centre of gravity in my body. Both the breath and the bodyscan meditations can be done while walking.

Meditating with your eyes open can be difficult at first. Our eyes usually hop from attraction to attraction like summer flies. They continually scan the entire scene with small movements we are rarely aware of. When we are anxious, the muscles that swivel the eyeballs tighten, the eyes move faster and the brainwaves stay in beta.

So try to switch off the "eyeball-swivelling" muscles and let your eyes go still in the sockets. It may help to hook the eyes on a point in the distance — a tree or car — and reel yourself in towards it. This keeps your head centred and helps you resist glancing sideways.

Try to recall how your eyes feel when you are gazing at a sunset, enjoying a painting, or looking at someone you love. They usually feel soft and gentle. The alpha brainwaves are present. Recreate that kind of feeling in your eyes as you walk.

Walking is just a posture, like sitting, in which you can practise any meditation. When you feel grounded in basic walking meditation, it is possible to branch out from it. Rather than focusing on the body in movement, we can consciously focus on other things. It is often best to name your object like a mantra as you breathe out, to keep on track. Here are some possibilities:

1. "Sound". As you walk, consciously explore the sound-scape that comes and goes around you. Hold the sounds in your mind a little after they fade. You can also do this with "smell" (good in suburban streets around teatime) or "sight".

2. "Sensing". Let your mind dwell a moment on any sense object that takes your attention. Let things arise and pass spontaneously. Your mind will automatically be drawn to this or that: a cat on a post, a puddle, a bug, the smell of petrol fumes, a woman's skirt, and so on. If you are consciously sensing, you are in the meditation. But draw your mind back when it disappears into thought.

3. "Colour". Notice which colours attract you. In a glance take in the shade and hue of an object without investigating it. Extract the colour and imprint it in your mind, so you can carry it for a few yards once the object leaves your field of vision.

4. "Wind". Focus primarily on the air moving over your face as you walk. This is a beautiful practice even in the absence of any breeze.

5. "Space". Say the word "space" as you take in the feeling of the sky above. Internalise it. Imagine your body becoming spacious.

6. "Light". Notice the quality of light everywhere. Don't focus on the trees themselves, but on the light glittering through them. Don't focus on the building but on

the light shining off it. As in the "space" meditation, internalise the light so you feel yourself shining from within.

7. "Peace". Feel yourself walking in harmony with yourself and the world. Let your footsteps be peaceful on the earth. You could also use any other mantra or affirmation.

8. At night-time, when you do a sitting meditation, mentally recall the objects that stood out during your day's walking meditation. Savour again the feeling of each one.

The basic guidelines for any meditation still apply for those outlined above: be relaxed, focus on one thing, bring the mind back when it wanders. The art of meditation is consciously to bring one part of your experience into the foreground, and let the rest remain in the background. Walking meditations can easily dissolve into a pleasant meander unless we are careful. When meditating we still need to know where the mind is from moment to moment.

I suggest you be systematic to get the most from these meditations. It is said that a piece of information needs to be taken in four times before it moves from short-term into long-term memory. You might have noticed that principle with phone numbers. Similarly meditation teachers say that any exercise needs to be done at least three times over three days to be embedded in the mind. After that, you can pick it up again at any time.

Walking meditation takes your practice into the streets. It balances the introspective tendencies of sitting. This usually gives us a deeper empathy with nature and we feel more at ease in the world at large.

# CHAPTER SEVENTEEN

# DEEP HEALING

We occasionally hear of "miracle" cures through meditation. These are rare, but do happen. In the East, terminally ill people often say good-bye to their families and go to a monastery to die. A few, however, are still alive years later, hale and hearty.

Such people rarely return to their former lives. The cure happened because there was a "deep turning in the seat of consciousness". Their meditations were not a kind of psychic surgery that cut out their illness leaving the rest of the body/mind intact. Everything changed.

I promised myself, as I wrote this book, that I would only talk about things I could adequately explain in the space available. This is a book for beginners, after all. In this chapter, I break that rule. Deep healing is "post-graduate" work, so I apologise if this outline raises more questions than it answers. However, I thought it best at least to sketch in the process.

The causes of stress seem to be manifold. We might blame poor health, working or living conditions, difficulties in relationships, our upbringing or our unnatural modern lifestyle. But there is a more fundamental cause. It is in the way we react.

If we react negatively, we squirm like a worm on a hook, trapped by fear, anger or desire. If we react positively, life is tolerable if not always pleasant. People can find great serenity and bliss in concentration camps, prisons or during war. But others are paralysed with anxiety in the midst of trouble-free lives. Whether we live in heaven or hell depends largely on our responses to life.

The source of most stress is blocked or frozen emotion. It often occurs when we live a lie. In fact any emotion, in its basic impulse, is actually positive. The problem only arises when it is blocked either by ourselves or by outer circumstances.

Blocking emotion is a good and necessary short-term strategy. We have all been doing it since birth — and maybe before. But the emotion doesn't vanish: it goes underground. It is always trying to surface, even if it is decades old. If it can't come through as emotion, it may erupt as sickness in the body.

Emotions are very physical things. Each is a precise cocktail of hormones that creates immediate results in the body. It is useful to see emotions as moving either up or down. Anger is a hard upward movement. Joy is a soft upward movement. Fear is a hard downward movement. Sorrow is a soft downward movement.

The word "emotion" originally meant "to move out". If

we don't block an emotion, it moves through and physical equilibrium returns. However the process is like a fever. It can be painful and can completely incapacitate us for a while. A person surrendering to grief, anger or desire is unable to work or get the kids off to school.

Furthermore, most full expressions of emotion will not be tolerated by the people around you (rightly so, I might add. Most strong emotion is blind). If you vent your rage fully, for example, your body may feel satisfied, but the outer consequences could be catastrophic.

So we freeze it or leak it out in smaller doses. Unfortunately the deep freeze can overload and break down in time. I analysed a dream recently in which exactly this image arose. A woman dreamt she found a dismembered corpse in the bottom of her estranged husband's refrigerator. She instinctively knew it related to the way she "froze up" when her marriage collapsed. She also felt it related to her recurring skin cancers.

If we look at the emotional tone of our thoughts, we can see if they will lead to happiness or misery. There is a simple guideline here. An unhealthy thought makes the mind tight, narrow and obsessed. A healthy thought makes the mind loose, open and receptive to new things.

If you can't tell the difference, look at your body. Ask yourself whether a particular thought makes your body feel tight and painful, or loose and open. An emotion doesn't just occur in your mind. It is a physical event also. The body both mirrors thoughts and emotions and bears the consequences of them. The next time you get angry, for example, take a moment to observe the accompanying sensations in your body. The chances are they will be quite uncomfortable.

We often find that thoughts we indulge willingly are physically painful: our self-righteous pet hates, for example, or our desire for something unattainable. Thoughts alone can make our stomachs knot up, our blood pressure rise and our breathing spasmodic. People can literally "worry themselves sick", to the point of getting a headache or vomiting.

Feelings of aversion (fear, anger, sorrow, resentment) or attraction (desire, possessiveness) shrink the whole world to the size of a pinhead. In those moments, nothing is more important than that sexy body or that grievous insult. Unhealthy emotion makes the mind small and obsessed. The body tightens and squirms on the hook. And when the hook goes through us, disease may occur.

By meditating, we observe our quality of mind. It is like testing water: it may look pure, but closer examination may show it to be laced with unhealthy emotion. Many people who try to be good are consumed by the emotions they are trying to avoid. Just as people in third world countries can survive with contaminated water, so we can get by with contaminated minds. But our quality of life and our health may be terrible.

Mindstates and emotions come and go rapidly. Our work is to recognise and release the unhealthy ones quickly, and to boost the healthy ones. This is our life's task. It is not easy. For one thing, we often don't know the difference between the healthy and the unhealthy. And yet nothing we do is more important than this. The beginning and end of body/mind health and the spiritual path is right here.

Meditating teaches us tolerance. At first, we learn to cope with the barking dog, the sore back, the aggravation at work. The pain may still be there, but we no longer pick at the scab. Gradually this acceptance extends to bigger things. It can be quite a surprise to find yourself not getting upset or angry when you usually would. These are called the "non-signs" of accomplishment. It is as if part of your identity is dropping away.

The memory of a brutal parent may arise, for example, and you realise it no longer triggers off your habitual resentment. This is a sign that the old emotion has worked its way through, without a trace or afterthought remaining. Dropping such negativities is very healthy for both mind and body.

It is easy to say "I forgive" without feeling it. Real healing occurs when not just your mind but the instinctive responses in your body become peaceful. There may be a tangible flow of love and sympathetic understanding towards those who apparently wronged us. After all, we usually know them well enough to know how much they are suffering themselves.

Big liberations are often based on thousands of tiny shifts in both body and mind. These shifts may be quite unexpected. Blocked emotion may well surface as strange sensations in the body. Let me describe this process.

When we are tranquil, our minds may start throwing out the garbage. It is like the way a body throws off toxins when we go on a fast — and the symptoms can be similar. Uncomfortable sensations may suddenly arise for no apparent reason. They may pass through as waves of discomfort: itching, nausea, faintness, palpitations, trembling, shooting pains, flushes, feeling bloated or lopsided, restless, and so on.

Although these are usually quite subtle, they can be difficult to sit through. They are usually unacknowledged emotions surfacing on the physical plane. People often feel something is wrong with their meditation and stop. This is a mistake. Their meditation is actually bearing fruit.

The challenge is to just watch. A sensation triggered by an emotional shift is different from a purely "physical" sensation. It is more like an intense memory resonating through the body. Unlike a backache caused by bad posture, for example, it may come and go in a flash. It may appear purely physical, but it is often accompanied by an unpleasant emotion as well.

If we can stay open to the feeling, its power over us is broken. It is freed and we are freed from it. It may return again, but with less strength. There may be flashes of great joy and lightness as these moments pass by, like the relief of a thorn being extracted.

These sensations are collectively called "bliss" because they indicate a deep rebalancing of the psyche. The blockages are dissolving. The lifeforce is moving through you. This process of deep inner cleansing may go on intermittently for years.

The deeper the meditation, the deeper the healing. At the risk of appearing mystical, let me describe some deeper states of consciousness.

The word "samadhi" means absorption, or oneness. We get little tastes of it outside meditation, for example when we are so absorbed in the beauty of nature, or music, or occasionally in sport or dance or lovemaking, that time stands still and everything shines with an inner light. Samadhi is like the most transcendent moment of that experience.

In such moments all sense of self vanishes. What remains of "you" is simply pure awareness. In those moments, you don't know your name, age, sex or the century you live in. Yet absorption is a state of exceptional clarity and bliss — it is not a blank-out. As it often lasts only a few seconds you are unlikely to get lost there.

In samadhi, unhealthy emotion vanishes utterly, like snowflakes in a fire. There is no self there to be hurt, so fear and anger disappear. Not the slightest aversion or attraction, conscious or unconscious, can get a foothold.

Paradoxically, full absorption only arises when "you" stop trying to achieve it. All desire has to go too. "Don't try to awaken" they say in Soto Zen. "Just sit". When the negativities are dropped, the breakthroughs can happen.

Absorption happens when "you" vanish into the object. If you remain there, a strange thing happens: the object vanishes, too. There is simply infinite space. You were one with the breath, now you are one with nothing. There is just watching, like a mirror reflecting the sky. You are like a cat at a mouse hole, intensely alert. But even the cat has gone. You have entered the background vibration of pure consciousness itself.

Paradoxically, this state is always with us, though we rarely see it plainly. It is like the background hum of the Big Bang resonating through the universe. The mind we do the dishes with is the same as that which sees God.

In this state, the mind becomes unified. This is no small matter. The psychic energy, usually scattered, now all streams in one direction, like iron shavings on a magnetised iron bar. The longer we stay in this state, the more deeply it transforms us. It affects mind, body and emotions equally.

Samadhi may be felt physically as a streaming, almost liquid, light. It is described as the nectar of the gods, "like sugarcane juice" melting the bound energies in the spinal column. Other people may feel it as a blissful heat or fire. It is described as the inner sacrificial fire that consumes every obstacle to liberation.

When the mind unifies, you are one with everything imaginable. Nothing is excluded. You feel one with God, with nature, with all humanity (including those you hate.) You are no longer at war with yourself or anyone or anything. Even your suffering is perfect in its own way. Nothing is lacking. In these moments what else could you possibly want?

When the negatives disappear, the positives are naturally there in full force. As Jampolsky, an American therapist, says "Love is letting go of fear". Samadhi is a state of boundless love, joy and acceptance.

Samadhi is an extremely healthy, life-affirming state of mind. We no longer send out the emotional signals that support chronic disease in the body. This is when cancers may start to dissolve, or the grief and anger of decades may disintegrate.

Yet samadhi by itself doesn't cure. It just indicates that the person is capable of dropping the negatives. Certainly, this is no small achievement, but unless the person is also inspired to turn their life around outside the meditation, a cure is unlikely.

Healing requires a clearing of all negativity, not just in the meditation but in daily life. Every narrowminded thought is a nail in the coffin. All our pet obsessions, our nice ways of being nasty, our habitual gripes, drive us into the grave. It becomes essential to "make peace", at least in our hearts, with all the trials of our life, both the people and the events, whether they are present or in the distant past. Not a quick and easy thing to do!

Meditation, as a tool for self-awareness, will help you see what your thought patterns are doing to you. This may give you the impetus and courage to change. From the first moment we sit to meditate, we boost the positive states of mind. Each time we relax, our fears, anger and desires subside. The samadhi states deepen this process enormously.

I will conclude this chapter with some suggestions for people who are seriously ill. As my teacher says, this is all of us. We all carry the seeds of illness and death, and it is just a matter of time before they ripen. So these comments actually apply to everyone.

Deep healing requires a fundamental shift in consciousness. To be given a death sentence from a doctor often shocks people into a total re-evaluation of themselves. They may well stop work and go to a beach cottage or a health farm for weeks to "take stock". This is meditation in the Western sense of "thinking deeply about something". Whether they die or not, their lives change.

If you have AIDS or cancer or are otherwise looking death in the face, meditation will help. A little meditation will help a little. A lot of meditation will help a lot. I would recommend at least two or three hours a day of meditation or some well-focused activity.

The quality of meditation will be the crucial factor. To relax and let the mind wander is of limited value. To enter samadhi, or to develop the clarity to notice negative states of mind arising, will require much practice and, almost certainly, training with a teacher or group. It is harder and slower, and for many people, impossible to achieve good results alone.

If you are quite sick, you probably don't have the time to figure out for yourself how to meditate well. I strongly recommend you train and practise with others.

It may be necessary to make major changes in your lifestyle. If your work envelops you in negativity, get out of it. Give yourself time to think and be, even if it means leaving your family for a few weeks.

Give yourself the opportunity, and the therapeutic support if you need it, to be emotional. Healing involves cleaning out the emotional basement and there may be a lot of junk there. We need to feel our suffering, but at the same time watch it with detachment. It is quite difficult to maintain this balance. Meditation can help you see clearly and fully without being swept away by emotion. Beat cushions by all means, but do it with awareness.

The bottom line in all of this is: eradicate the negatives, whenever they arise. And boost the positives. And
know the difference between them. That is all. Nothing
else matters.

If you are facing death and want to do the best for
yourself, I would suggest:

1. Meditate long and deeply.
2. Create time and space to re-evaluate everything.
3. Allow the frozen emotions through, with awareness.
4. Be prepared to change your lifestyle and attitudes.

# RECOMMENDED READING

## Books on Meditation

Greer Allica, *Meditation Workbook*, David Lovell Publishing, Melbourne, 1990.

Ram Dass, *Journey of Awakening*, Bantam, New York, 1978.

Shakti Gawain, *Creative Visualisation*, Bantam, New York, 1982.

Ian Gawler, *Peace of Mind*, Hill of Content, Melbourne, 1987.

Arthur Hough, *Dynamic Silence*, CompCare Publishers, Minneapolis, 1991.

Jon Kabat-Zinn, *Full Catastrophe Living*, Dell Publishing, New York, 1990.

Laurence LeShan, *How to Meditate*, Aquarian Press, 1993.

Joel Levey, *The Fine Arts of Relaxation, Concentration and Meditation*, Wisdom Publications, London, 1987.

Stephen Levine, *A Gradual Awakening*, Gateway Books, 1992.

Michael Page, *Visualisation*, The Aquarian Press, 1990.

Osho Rajneesh, *Meditation: The First and Last Freedom*, The Rebel Publishing House, Cologne.

Jose Silva, *The Silva Mind Control Method*, Panther, 1980.

## Books on Buddhist Meditation

Joseph Goldstein and Jack Kornfield, *Seeking the Heart of Wisdom*, Shambhala, Boston, 1987.

Jack Kornfield, *Living Buddhist Masters*, Unity Press, Santa Cruz, 1977.

Lama Anagarika Govinda, *Foundations of Tibetan Mysticism*, Samuel Weiser, New York, 1969.

Lama Anagarika Govinda, *The Way of the White Clouds*, Rider, 1992.

Shunryu Suzuki, *Zen Mind, Beginners Mind*, Weatherhill, New York, 1986.

Tarthang Tulku, *Gesture of Balance*, Dharma Publications, Berkeley, 1977.

Thich Nhat Hanh, *The Miracle of Mindfulness*, Paralax, Berkeley, 1984.

Thich Nhat Hanh, *A Guide to Walking Meditation*, Paralax, Berkeley, 1985.

Chogyam Trungpa, *Cutting Through Spiritual Materialism*, Shambhala, Berkeley, 1973.

Alan Watts, *The Way of Zen*, Arkana, 1991.

# ACKNOWLEDGEMENTS

Few of the ideas in this book are my own. I am indebted to most of the writers listed in the last chapter. I even find it hard to regard this book as 'mine'. Millions of people before me have meditated and shared what they know. I hope this book will spread this wisdom on to others.

My thanks are also due to the thousands of students and friends who have supported me over the years. I often wonder 'Who is teaching who?' It has been a great delight and privilege to explore the human psyche with them.

Finally I wish to thank my parents, Noel and Val Harrison, for their help and support throughout my life. I dedicate this book to them.

# INDEX